ELIZABETH COLEMAN first came to attention with her dark comedy *It's My Party (And I'll Die If I Want To)* which premiered at the 1993 Melbourne Comedy Festival and has been regularly produced ever since. In 1999 Elizabeth's next play, *Secret Bridesmaids' Business*, broke box office records in Melbourne before embarking on a triumphant national tour in 2000 and being adapted into a telemovie, produced by Linda House for ABC Television. *Secret Bridesmaids' Business* has also been produced many times, including a musical production in Tokyo by Takarazuka Creative Arts. Elizabeth's comedy about love gone wrong, *This Way Up*, premiered in Melbourne in 2001. Elizabeth has also written many screenplays for television, most recently 'Miss Fisher's Murder Mysteries'. She co-created and co-wrote the popular drama series 'Bed of Roses', with Jutta Goetze, for Southern Star and ABC Television. *Almost with You* premiered at Melbourne's La Mama Theatre in 2012.

SECRET *bridesmaids'* BUSINESS

&

IT'S MY PARTY
(And I'll Die If I Want To)

CURRENCY PRESS
SYDNEY

Elizabeth Coleman

Secret Bridesmaids' Business was first published by Currency Press, PO Box 2287, Strawberry Hills NSW 2012, in association with Playbox Theatre in 1999.
It's My Party (And I'll Die If I Want To) was first published in *The La Mama Collection* by Currency Press in 1997.
This revised edition published in 2011.
Reprinted 2014, 2015, 2016, 2018
Copyright © Elizabeth Coleman, *Secret Bridesmaids' Business* 2003, 2011; *It's My Party (And I'll Die If I Want To)* 1993, 2011.

COPYING FOR EDUCATIONAL PURPOSES

The Australian *Copyright Act 1968* (Act) allows a maximum of one chapter or 10% of this book, whichever is the greater, to be copied by any educational institution for its educational purposes provided that that educational institution (or the body that administers it) has given a remuneration notice to Copyright Agency Limited (CAL) under the Act.
For details of the CAL licence for educational institutions contact CAL, 11/66 Goulburn Street, Sydney, NSW, 2000; tel: within Australia 1800 066 844 toll free; outside Australia 61 2 9394 7600; fax: 61 2 9394 7601; email: info@copyright.com.au

COPYING FOR OTHER PURPOSES

Except as permitted under the Act, for example a fair dealing for the purposes of study, research, criticism or review, no part of this book may be reproduced, stored in a retrieval system, or transmitted in any form or by any means without prior written permission. All enquiries should be made to the publisher at the above address.

Any performance or public reading of *Secret Bridesmaids' Business or It's My Party (And I'll Die If I Want To)* is forbidden unless a licence has been received from the author or the author's agent. The purchase of this book in no way gives the purchaser the right to perform the play in public, whether by means of a staged production or a reading. All applications for public performance should be made to the author, c/o Cameron's Management, Locked Bag 848, Surry Hills NSW 2010; ph +61 2 9319 7199; email info@cameronsmanagement.com.au

Cataloguing-in-publication data for this title is available from the National Library of Australia website.
Typeset by Dean Nottle for Currency Press.
Cover design by Emma Vine for Currency Press.

Currency Press acknowledges the Traditional Owners of the Country on which we live and work. We pay our respects to all Aboriginal and Torres Strait Islander Elders, past and present.

Contents

SECRET BRIDESMAIDS' BUSINESS
    Act One   5
    Act Two   52

IT'S MY PARTY (AND I'LL DIE IF I WANT TO)
    Act One   99
    Act Two   135

SECRET
bridesmaids'
BUSINESS

Secret Bridesmaids' Business was first produced by Playbox Theatre Centre at The C.U.B. Malthouse, Melbourne, on 14 April 1999, with the following cast:

COLLEEN BACON	Joan Sydney
MEG BACON	Ulli Birvé
ANGELA DIXON	Tara Morice
LUCY DEAN	Kate Johnston
NAOMI BARTLETT	Rachael Beck
JAMES DAVIS	Fred Whitlock

Director, Catherine Hill
Designer, Shaun Gurton
Lighting Designer, Andrew Livingston
Executive Director, Aubrey Mellor

CHARACTERS

COLLEEN BACON, 55-plus, the bride's mother. Flustered, bossy, well-intentioned.

MEG BACON, 33, the bride. Smart, warm, fun.

ANGELA DIXON, 34, the Matron of Honour. Loyal, giving, occasionally vague.

LUCY DEAN, 34, Bridesmaid. Earthy, impetuous, direct.

NAOMI BARTLETT, 28, a friend. Sexy, self-absorbed, conflicted.

JAMES DAVIS, 35, the bridegroom. Successful, confident, sincere.

HOTEL HOUSEMAID

SETTING

Secret Bridesmaids' Business takes place in a hotel suite in the hours leading up to Meg Bacon's wedding. Meg's gathered together her mum and her bridesmaids for one last night of good old-fashioned girlie fun—well, that's the plan, anyway.

ACT ONE

SCENE ONE

It's early evening. We're in an elegant hotel, around four-star standard. The room contains a double bed, a single bed, a table with four chairs, a TV, a sofa, a mirror, a mini-bar. The usual stuff. A muted city view shows through a window. It's dusk.

There is a door leading off, upstage, to the bathroom and another door, stage right, which leads to the connecting bedroom. Another door, stage left, leads out into the hotel corridor. Overnight bags lie around the room, open and partly unpacked.

A covered wedding dress and a covered bridesmaid's dress are hanging in the wardrobe. We can see the flowing folds of a veil hanging beside them.

A dozen yellow roses in a vase and a large roll of silver ribbon sit on the table.

A woman in her mid to late fifties, COLLEEN, *is talking on the phone. She's clearly enjoying her state of flustered agitation.*

COLLEEN: [*into the phone*] Seventeen vegetarians?! But we've only got sixteen pumpkin and fetta flans! Why didn't you—? What? An *hour* ago?! Well, what are we going to— ? Oh, alright, that sounds like a good solution—but you're sure you've got spare asparagus spears? Good. Now, you will let me know if there are any more problems? Alright. 'Bye— [*Calling towards the bathroom without pausing for breath*] Meg! Why didn't you tell me that Naomi Bartlett's boyfriend's a vegetarian?!

MEG: [*off*] What?

COLLEEN: I said why didn't you tell me that Naomi Bartlett's boyfriend is a vegetarian?!

The bathroom door opens and MEG *enters. She's attractive, thirty-three. She has a line of white bleach above her upper lip. As this conversation takes place she walks to the table and picks up the roll of silver ribbon.*

MEG: Naomi hasn't got a boyfriend.
COLLEEN: Well, who's this man she's bringing to the wedding, then?

MEG: I don't know. I think it's some guy she met at Pilates.
COLLEEN: *Some guy she met at—?!* So you're telling me that a total stranger is taking up a place that could've gone to your Great Uncle Reg?
MEG: Mum, we've been through this a million times. I haven't seen Uncle Reg since 1997.
COLLEEN: But you've never even met this vegetarian man.
MEG: M-u-u-u-u-m…
COLLEEN: It's all very well for you to take that tone. You're not the one who had to ring Uncle Reg.
MEG: And did Uncle Reg give a rat's arse?
COLLEEN: [*language*] Meg!
MEG: [*overlapping*] Is this the ribbon for the pews?
COLLEEN: Yes, I had to get that one because they'd run out of the—
MEG: [*overlapping*] But it's too thick.
COLLEEN: Too what? Too *thick?*
MEG: Too *wide*. I told you I wanted it fine, remember? This one looks like… gaffer tape.
COLLEEN: [*hiding worry*] It does not look like gaffer tape! They only had twenty-one metres in the width you wanted and I wasn't going to have half the pews with one width and half the pews with another.
MEG: But we could've put the elegant ribbons up the front and the others on the back pews. No-one would've noticed—

> *The door opens and another woman* MEG'*s age enters. She's* ANGELA. *She carries a cardboard box that contains place cards for the reception.*

COLLEEN: I'm not having the church look untidy, Meg. There's nothing wrong with this ribbon!
MEG: [*mildly*] Alright, okay… [*The place cards:*] That them, Ange?
ANGELA: [*nodding*] Yeah. The receptionist put them away and then went off duty. But they found them eventually.

> *She hands the box to* COLLEEN, *who opens it. Meanwhile* MEG *takes out her mobile phone.*

COLLEEN: Thank you, Angela. What do *you* think of that ribbon? It's not too wide to make a nice bow, is it?

> ANGELA *takes the ribbon.* MEG *is punching a number into her mobile.*

MEG: Mum, forget the ribbon. It's fine, really... [*To* ANGELA] I just have to give Rache a quick call—

ANGELA *nods, still studying the ribbon. But* COLLEEN*'s moved on to another crisis.*

COLLEEN: Oh no! We can't use these!
MEG: [*stopping dialling*] What?!
COLLEEN: These name cards! They're not folded properly!
ANGELA: What do you mean—?
COLLEEN: [*overlapping*] Well, look! [*Holding up some name cards, she reads.*] 'Thank you for sharing our special d'. You can't see the rest of the word!
ANGELA: Oh no...
COLLEEN: We'll have to re-fold them!
MEG: Show me. Oh, they *are* a bit crooked...
COLLEEN: *A bit?!* They're a dog's breakfast! Come and help me fold them—

She bustles over to the dining table, revelling in this latest crisis. ANGELA *dutifully follows. Satisfied that things are under control,* MEG *resumes punching numbers into her mobile.*

Meg, I need you too.
MEG: I just want to ring Rache. Can I do that first?
COLLEEN: This will take five minutes. Come on, quickly.

MEG *knows better than to argue. She puts her mobile back in her pocket and heads over to* COLLEEN *and* ANGELA *at the table.* ANGELA*'s already started folding.*

MEG: [*travelling*] But this means the place cards will have two creases.
COLLEEN: I know. I'm livid!
MEG: But don't you think that'll look a bit tacky?
COLLEEN: It'll look a lot better than the way they are now!
MEG: I don't know. Ange, what do you think—?
COLLEEN: Your father and I didn't pay all that money for crooked name cards. Here, quickly— [*Handing out cards, demonstrating*] Now make sure you join the bottom corners evenly... like that...
ANGELA: [*holding up a perfectly folded card*] Like that, Mrs Bacon?
COLLEEN: Good. That's it.

MEG *reads a name card aloud, smiling at* ANGELA.

MEG: Ah, John Dixon. Think I know him... Good-looking guy with a gorgeous wife, right?
ANGELA: That's him. Where's he sitting?
MEG: At—
COLLEEN: [*over her*] Table Eleven.
MEG: Yeah, with Louise and Ben and Sue and Jack and Naomi and, ah, her friend...
COLLEEN: See? You don't even know the man's name.

> MEG *pulls a playful face at her mother. Meanwhile* ANGELA *looks at the seating plan.*

ANGELA: Oh, next to Ben. That's good. He likes Ben.
COLLEEN: Are the children staying with John's parents, Angela?
ANGELA: [*nodding*] Till Sunday morning...
COLLEEN: All the way till Sunday?
ANGELA: Yeah...
MEG: Oh, Ange, are you missing them already?
ANGELA: As if!

> *They all smile.*

Not yet, anyway.
MEG: You know, Holly's growing up so quickly...
ANGELA: I know... Scary, isn't it?
MEG: Remember we always used to say that our kids would play together? At this rate yours are going to babysit mine.
COLLEEN: Still, Sweetheart, better late than never.
MEG: Yeah... If I have three in the next three or four years, I'll still be pretty much on target.
ANGELA: Three in three years?
MEG: Well, you know what they say, the risk of pregnancy complications increases dramatically after thirty-five.
ANGELA: Oh, I don't know... We know heaps of girls who had their first baby in their late thirties.
MEG: Yeah, but they only had *one*—I want at least three.
ANGELA: It's going to be a bit of a juggle with work...
MEG: That's why I got Rache on board. I've been all about work for too long, Ange. It's time. I want some little kids under my feet, giving me the shits.

> ANGELA *laughs, but* COLLEEN *looks mildly shocked.*

COLLEEN: Oh, Sweetheart, they'll bring you more joy than you can possibly imagine.

    MEG *nods, glowing—she* can *imagine.*

ANGELA: Meg, how long have you had that bleach on?

MEG: Oh, my God. I forgot! My upper lip's going to be red raw! [*Jumping to her feet*] Why didn't you say something, Mum?

    MEG*'s mobile starts ringing.*

COLLEEN: I can't remember *everything—*

MEG: [*answering her phone*] Hey, Rache—I was just about to call you. Can you give me two seconds?

    She hurriedly exits to the bathroom with the phone.

COLLEEN: [*to* ANGELA] Speaking of remembering things—what happened with your shoes?

    ANGELA *looks like she'd rather not discuss this topic. She tries to fob* COLLEEN *off.*

ANGELA: My shoes were fine. Look, this place card's even more crooked than the others—

COLLEEN: [*overlapping*] Oh, of course, it was Lucy's. What happened in the end?

    ANGELA *tries to play the whole thing down.*

ANGELA: Well, the woman couldn't find the right fabric to cover them because it was coming from Singapore, and so she—

COLLEEN: [*overlapping*] Thailand.

ANGELA: Yeah, that's right. Thailand. And they only had enough fabric for mine, but in the end it was all— [sorted out.]

COLLEEN: [*interrupting, alarmed*] They found some though, didn't they? I thought they'd found the fabric.

ANGELA: Yeah, they did. And it's almost exactly the same. You know, I can't seem to fold this one properly—

COLLEEN: [*interrupting*] Almost? You mean it's not the same fabric?!

ANGELA: [*oops*] Well, not technically. But it's exactly the same colour.

COLLEEN: [*alarm bells ringing*] It's not shiny, is it?

ANGELA: Well, it's just, it's just maybe got the *tiniest hint* of a sheen—

COLLEEN: [*interrupting*] But your shoes have got a matt finish!

ANGELA: Yeah, I know, but you can hardly see it—

COLLEEN: [*overlapping*] Why didn't Meg tell me this?!
ANGELA: Ah, I'm not sure that Lucy's mentioned it to her…
COLLEEN: What?!
ANGELA: I don't think she thought it was that important.
COLLEEN: But she's going to be devastated.
ANGELA: It's okay, Mrs Bacon. They look just like mine.
COLLEEN: But how can they, if they're shiny?!

> ANGELA *is rendered speechless. What can one possibly say in the face of such disaster?*

I told Meg to organise Lucy's shoes but no, she had to leave it to her—and now this!
ANGELA: I really don't think it's going to matter that much—

> *But* COLLEEN *is marching over to the bathroom door, calling out briskly.*

COLLEEN: Meg! There's a problem with Lucy's shoes—!

> *The bathroom door opens and* MEG *re-emerges, bleach removed. She's still engrossed in her phone call with Rachel.*

MEG: [*into the phone*] That's the perfect spot for that photo shoot. Who did you pitch the story to? Fantastic! We'll get page five with him—
COLLEEN: [*interrupting, in crisis mode*] Meg! Lucy's shoes!
MEG: [*into the phone*] Good for you, Rache—I've got to go, 'bye. [*She hangs up.*] What…?
COLLEEN: Lucy's shoes! The fabric's different to Angela's!
MEG: What do you mean, different?
COLLEEN: It's shiny!
MEG: Shiny?
ANGELA: It's not *that* shiny—
MEG: [*overlapping*] But Angela's shoes are matt!
COLLEEN: *I* know that!
ANGELA: You can hardly see it. Really. If you could notice it, Lucy would have mentioned it.
COLLEEN: This is so typical of Lucy, causing trouble like this.
MEG: M-u-u-u-m… [*Turning to* ANGELA] Can you really not see it?
ANGELA: Really. If I hadn't told you, you probably wouldn't have even noticed.

> *At this moment there is a knock at the door.*

COLLEEN: Oh, I would've noticed.
LUCY: [*calling from outside*] It's me!
MEG: Speak of the devil. [*Calling as she walks to the door*] Are your ears burning, Luce?

> *She opens the door.* LUCY *enters. She's tall, striking, thirty-four. She carries an overnight bag.*

LUCY: Huh…?

> MEG *and* LUCY *squeal in a 'girlie' fashion as they give each other a great big hug. Then:*

[*Entering*] Hi, Angela, Colleen—
COLLEEN: [*overlapping*] Lucy, show me your shoes.
LUCY: What—?
COLLEEN: Can you show me your shoes, please? Quickly.

> *Misunderstanding her,* LUCY *gives her a funny look and holds out her foot.*

No, not those. Your bridesmaid's shoes.
LUCY: Oh, right—
MEG: Mum, how about saying hello?
COLLEEN: I'm sorry. Hello, Lucy. Angela tells me your shoes are shiny.

> LUCY *gets them out of her bag, throwing a* 'thanks a lot' *look at* ANGELA.

ANGELA: That's not exactly what I said—
LUCY: They're not *very* shiny—
MEG: Why didn't you tell me?
LUCY: Because you can't even notice the difference.
COLLEEN: Well, I certainly hope you're right.
ANGELA: She is, really.
COLLEEN: Can you get me one of your shoes, Angela?

> *As* ANGELA *walks at a normal pace,* COLLEEN *barks at her:*

Quickly!

> ANGELA *reluctantly hurries to the wardrobe and grabs a shoe. She brings it back to* COLLEEN. *Meanwhile* COLLEEN *and* MEG *peer at* LUCY*'s shoe under a desk light.*

It's definitely shiny!

LUCY: You can hardly notice.
MEG: You can notice *a bit*...

> LUCY *looks like she's trying to contain deep tension.*

COLLEEN: [*grabbing* ANGELA'*s shoe*] Here, let me see—
ANGELA: See? They're no different—

> COLLEEN *holds up both shoes. They all peer at them as she gasps in horror.*

COLLEEN: They're chalk and cheese!
LUCY: Oh, they are not!
COLLEEN: Look at them! They don't match at all!
LUCY: [*a spontaneous outburst*] Oh, what a load of crap!
MEG: Lucy! She didn't mean that, Mum. She's just a bit—
LUCY: [*interrupting*] Sorry. Sorry, Colleen. I got caught in traffic. I'm stressed out. Sorry.
COLLEEN: That's alright...

> *The younger women exchange glances as* COLLEEN *makes the most of her martyrdom.*

I just want everything to be nice for Meg, and I'm sorry if that upsets some people...
MEG: Mum... it doesn't. And everything's going to be perfect... [*To* ANGELA *and* LUCY] Isn't it?
ANGELA: Of course. It'll be a beautiful wedding, Mrs Bacon.

> *They turn to look at* LUCY *expectantly: Your turn. She obliges.*

LUCY: Yeah. It'll be great. And you really shouldn't worry about the shoes. No-one who matters will take any notice.
COLLEEN: Well, *I* took notice, but never mind...

> LUCY *bites back a response as* ANGELA *jumps in quickly to ease the tension.*

ANGELA: Lucy, we're re-folding the name cards. Here, come and help—

> *She sits at the table.* LUCY *sits too.*

LUCY: So, what are we doing—?

> *But before* ANGELA *can demonstrate,* COLLEEN *grabs the place cards from her hands.*

COLLEEN: Actually, Angela, I think I'll finish folding them in my room...

MEG: Are you okay, Mum?
LUCY: [*through gritted teeth*] Sorry, Colleen.
COLLEEN: [*ignoring* LUCY] I'm fine, Sweetheart. I just need some peace and quiet for a few minutes. Excuse me...

Martyrdom in full flight, COLLEEN *exits into the other bedroom.*

LUCY: Sorry, Meg. I didn't know it was such a big deal— [*Turning straight to* ANGELA] Why'd you tell her they were shiny—?
ANGELA: [*overlapping*] I didn't. Well, I didn't mean to—
MEG: [*suddenly interrupting*] Hey, where's your dress?
LUCY: In the car.
MEG: In the car?! What if someone steals it?!
LUCY: No-one's going to steal a fifteen-year-old Corolla.
MEG: I meant the dress!
LUCY: Okay. I'll go get it now. Angela, want to come with me?
ANGELA: [*surprised*] Me?
LUCY: Yeah. There's other stuff to carry too.
MEG: Where are you parked?
LUCY: Downstairs. In the basement.
MEG: [*with relief*] Oh...
LUCY: [*over her, to* ANGELA] Come on—
MEG: I'll come too.
LUCY: [*a little too quickly*] No, I just need Angela.

MEG *and* ANGELA *look at her in surprise.*

Come on, Angela.
MEG: [*grinning*] Oh, I get it. This is Secret Bridesmaids' Business.
LUCY: [*smiling*] Yeah.
ANGELA: [*first she's heard of it*] Oh, okay! [*To* MEG] Well, you stay put.
MEG: [*smiling*] I was going to have a shower, anyway—

A knock at the door.

Who's that?

MEG *answers it to a* HOTEL HOUSEMAID. *She's holding a bridesmaid's dress.*

Oh, hi...
HOUSEMAID: Is Miss Dean in here?
LUCY: Yeah, that's me.

HOUSEMAID: I hope it's alright, but you left your car door unlocked. We've had a few thefts lately, so I took this out for you. I hope you don't mind—
LUCY: [*grabbing it*] Yes I *do* mind! What if *I* wanted to go down and get it?!
ANGELA: Lucy!
MEG: No, that's nice of you. Thank you.
HOUSEMAID: I'm sorry if I shouldn't have—I didn't mean to upset anyone—
MEG: [*overlapping*] No, don't take any notice of her. Thanks a lot.
LUCY: [*approaching her*] Sorry—

> *The* HOUSEMAID *sees* LUCY *coming and virtually breaks into a run as she exits.*

[*Calling to the closed door*] Sorry.
MEG: Is there anyone else you'd like to offend while you're at it?
LUCY: Yeah, you. Have a shower. You stink.
MEG: [*sniffing her underarm*] I do not stink. Why don't you just say, 'Get lost. We want to talk Secret Bridesmaids' Business'?
LUCY: Get lost. We want to talk Secret Bridesmaids' Business.

> MEG *starts walking towards the bathroom.*

MEG: Fine—but just remember—if anyone ties inflated condoms to the front of James' car, they die.

> *And with a grin* MEG *exits into the bathroom, closing the door behind her.*
>
> LUCY *watches the door, waiting for it to close, then guides* ANGELA *to the far side of the room.* ANGELA*'s all smiles, anticipating a fun bridesmaids' secret.*

ANGELA: [*chirpily*] I didn't know we had Secret Bridesmaids' Business!
LUCY: [*overlapping, urgent, low*] Angela, listen to me—I think James has been having an affair.
ANGELA: [*loudly*] What?! [*Lowering her voice*] What did you say?
LUCY: I said James has been having an affair.

> ANGELA *is totally gobsmacked as the bathroom door opens and* MEG *re-emerges.*

MEG: It might help if I took my girlie stuff with me…

She picks up her toiletries bag. ANGELA *and* LUCY *smile at her in a really false, strangled kind of manner.* MEG*'s amused.*

God. You two are so bad at acting like you haven't got a secret. And no shaving cream on the windscreen, either.

She walks back into the bathroom and closes the door.

ANGELA: [*low*] You must have it wrong.
LUCY: [*low*] No I haven't. He's been sleeping with Naomi Bartlett!
ANGELA: Naomi Bartlett…? [*Realising*] You mean Naomi from Meg's old netball team? No way! She's a friend of hers.
LUCY: Huh. Meg *thinks* she is.

Then, suddenly, from the bathroom:

MEG: Well, *that's* just great!

LUCY *and* ANGELA *look startled: Did Meg hear? The bathroom door opens again and* MEG *re-emerges. But her tone is playful.*

I forgot my loofah!
LUCY: Huh—?
MEG: Did you two bring a loofah?
ANGELA: What?
MEG: A loofah. Have you got one?
LUCY: Who packs a loofah when they're only away for one night?
MEG: I'll take that as a no. Ange, you?
ANGELA: [*shaking her head*] Sorry.
MEG: [*joking*] Great. So how am I supposed to scrape the dead skin cells off my thighs?
LUCY: I could ring downstairs and get a cheese grater.

ANGELA *tries to laugh, but it comes out sounding forced and a little strangled.*

MEG: You okay there, Ange?
LUCY: Just piss off and have your shower. [*Playfully pushing her*] Go on.
MEG: Alright, alright… I'm going.

MEG *grins and exits into the bathroom.*

ANGELA: [*low*] Where did you hear this?!
LUCY: Naomi's sister-in-law is best friends with Kate at work, and we were reading this article about infidelity in *Marie Claire* this arvo, and Kate

tells me that her best friend's sister-in-law has been sleeping with a guy who's engaged—she didn't know that I knew Naomi—
ANGELA: [*overlapping*] But she could have lots of sisters-in-law—
LUCY: [*overlapping*] But she said Naomi's name—
ANGELA: [*overlapping*] Yeah, but, James isn't the only guy who's engaged—
LUCY: [*overlapping*] She said James' name too!
ANGELA: [*overlapping*] His surname?
LUCY: No, but—
ANGELA: [*interrupting*] Well, there you go. James is a pretty common name.
LUCY: Yeah, but Naomi told her sister-in-law that this guy is engaged to a *friend* of hers!

This does make things look pretty incriminating, but ANGELA *is desperate not to believe it.*

ANGELA: [*shaking her head*] No way… it must be somebody else…
LUCY: Who else could it be? And Kate reckons it went on for four months.
ANGELA: Four months?!
LUCY: Yeah. And it only ended two weeks ago!
ANGELA: Oh, it couldn't be him—
LUCY: [*interrupting*] But Naomi rang her sister-in-law on Tuesday, and she was crying because he's getting married this Saturday morning—*tomorrow!*

The sound of a toilet flushing can be heard. They both look towards the bathroom warily, then lower their voices yet again.

ANGELA: No, no way… Kate must have made a mistake…
LUCY: I don't see how—but she's going to talk to her friend tonight and try and find out this James guy's surname—
ANGELA: Who is? Kate?
LUCY: Yeah. And then she's going to ring me—
ANGELA: [*interrupting*] And what's she going to do?
LUCY: [*impatiently*] Just let me tell you! She's going to find out this guy's surname, and then she's going to ring me here on the mobile.
ANGELA: [*with mixed feelings*] Here?
LUCY: But she's tried to get hold of her friend a few times already and she hasn't been home, so let's just hope she comes back—because I'd rather tell Meg it's definitely him than just say it's a guy called James.

ANGELA: What?

> LUCY *registers the unspoken objection. Her response is very definite—no greys.*

LUCY: Well, we'll have to tell her, either way.

> ANGELA *is absorbing all this as the bathroom door re-opens and* MEG *emerges in a fluffy hotel bathrobe. She's undressed but she hasn't had her shower yet.*

MEG: So, have you sorted out the Secret Bridesmaids' Business?
LUCY/ANGELA: Yeah/Yep…
MEG: Great. I'll expect a huge surprise, then.

> *Blissfully unaware of the irony of her statement, she heads over to pick up a hair dryer, stopping to grin back at her friends.*

I bet James is in on this, isn't he? Sneaky boy…
ANGELA: Our lips are sealed!

> LUCY *and* ANGELA *laugh awkwardly.* MEG *grins at them, then wanders back into the bathroom and closes the door.*

> *The sound of the shower running can be heard throughout the following conversation.*

We can't tell her, Lucy.
LUCY: What?!
ANGELA: We can't tell her.
LUCY: We *have* to tell her.
ANGELA: But this is the biggest day of Meg's life. We can't ruin it for her—
LUCY: James has done that, not us.
ANGELA: Has he? We don't know for certain, Lucy—
LUCY: Oh, come on. A guy called James who's getting married tomorrow to a friend of Naomi's—?
ANGELA: Well, Naomi's probably got lots of friends—
LUCY: Oh, give me a break—
ANGELA: We can't do this to her—!
LUCY: [*overlapping, exasperated*] But she needs to know!
ANGELA: But what if she already does?
LUCY: Oh, what?!
ANGELA: Well, maybe James has told her everything—that's if there's anything to tell—maybe they've already sorted it out?

LUCY: No way. She would have told me.
ANGELA: Not necessarily. She wouldn't want you to think that James was a bastard.
LUCY: Huh. Too late for that.
ANGELA: Look, Lucy, I just don't think we've got the right to—
LUCY: [*interrupting, patronising*] Don't you think Meg's got the right to make an informed decision?
ANGELA: Maybe she already has.
LUCY: *Or*—maybe she's under the mistaken impression that she can trust the guy she's marrying?!

    ANGELA *takes a beat or two to muster her argument.*

ANGELA: Look, Lucy, I know you've been Meg's best friend since uni, but I've known her since we were *seven* and—
LUCY: [*overlapping*] Oh, we're not playing 'Who knows Meg the best', are we?
ANGELA: No, I'm just saying that she's been planning this ever since we were kids—she used to get in trouble for doodling designs of her wedding dress instead of doing her long division—!
LUCY: So—?!
ANGELA: And she's had red picked out as her bridesmaids' colour since we saw *Pretty Woman* in 1990!
LUCY: *So?!*
ANGELA: And when Paul left and she hit thirty she thought it'd never happen, but now it finally has—
LUCY: Jesus. This has got nothing to do with anything—
ANGELA: Lucy, she's got a ten-thousand-dollar engagement ring, a two-thousand-dollar wedding dress, one hundred people coming at one hundred dollars a head, cousins here from the UK, flowers and outfits and hire cars—not to mention a honeymoon in Paris and Venice—
LUCY: Can you hear what you're saying? It's just a party! And because of one stupid party being ruined, you're prepared to let her have a lifetime of misery.
ANGELA: Who are *you* to say she'll have a 'lifetime of misery'?
LUCY: I'm just trying to make you see—
ANGELA: And *you* might think this is a 'stupid party', but it's the most important day of Meg's life. So far—
LUCY: But that's all it is—*one bloody day!* What is it about this *one day* that turns sane people into raving lunatics?

ANGELA: So she's a raving lunatic now?
LUCY: No, she's the smartest person I've ever met. Who else could start their own PR firm and have clients like hers within, what, four years? She's so sharp she could do anything she wants—so *why* is she obsessing about satin shoes?
ANGELA: Because she loves her job, but it's not enough. She wants James, too.

> LUCY *snorts, disdainful of James.*

And she wants a *family*.

> LUCY *is momentarily silenced.*

You know how much she wants *lots of kids*. This could be her last chance.
LUCY: So you want her to have kids with the wrong guy?
ANGELA: I don't think it's our place to say he *is* the wrong guy.

> LUCY *snorts in disbelief again, then she takes a few deep breaths and tries another tack.*

LUCY: [*patronising*] Look, Angela, you're lucky. You met John when you were young and you've always been happy. But things aren't that simple for everyone—
ANGELA: [*overlapping*] Oh, please—
LUCY: [*overlapping*] I'm just saying, if a person's life has always gone smoothly, sometimes they don't understand how complicated things can get for—
ANGELA: [*overlapping angrily*] Yes, that's me, Lucy. I'm an old married woman, and my life is totally boring.
LUCY: I didn't say that.
ANGELA: But that's what you think.
LUCY: No it's not—
ANGELA: [*overlapping*] Don't insult me, Lucy. I know you think that.
LUCY: [*only half telling the truth*] No I don't.
ANGELA: [*only saying this because she's been pushed*] And why are you so keen to ruin Meg's wedding anyway? I reckon you're just *jealous*.
LUCY: Jealous?!
ANGELA: Well, *you* met James first—
LUCY: So? What's that got to do with anything—?
ANGELA: [*overlapping*] And you liked him—

LUCY: Oh, for *two* weeks, *two years ago!*
ANGELA: [*not really believing this*] Maybe you still do.
LUCY: So *I* want Meg to break up with James so *I* can have him?
ANGELA: [*sighing*] No, of course not, that's not what I'm saying. Look, I just meant—I don't know what I meant—I—
LUCY: [*interrupting*] I'm not the one who's been fucking the guy!

They hear the shower been turned off.

They both turn to look towards the bathroom, registering the sudden silence. They stare at each other angrily for a moment, then collect themselves and lower their voices.

ANGELA: Look, I'm sorry, Lucy, I didn't mean that, I'm sorry, but I just don't think we should… Look, can we agree to wait until Kate rings and we find out the guy's surname? Please?

LUCY thinks for a moment. This is a patently reasonable suggestion.

LUCY: But I'm not even sure that she'll definitely ring.
ANGELA: Well, can we put a time on it, then? Can we say that if Kate hasn't called by—I don't know—ten thirty, we'll talk about it again?

Again LUCY can't deny that this is a reasonable suggestion.

[*Pressing her advantage*] Wouldn't you rather know it's definitely him?
LUCY: [*after a beat*] Alright. What time is it now?
ANGELA: [*looking at her watch*] Quarter to eight.
LUCY: Quarter to eight. Okay, we'll give it till ten thirty, and if Kate hasn't rung, we'll re-assess.
ANGELA: So you promise you won't say anything to Meg until we've talked about it again?
LUCY: [*petulantly*] I promise.
ANGELA: Good.

LUCY and ANGELA stare at each other, at an impasse. The argument resolved (for now), they're back to where they've always been—two women with nothing in common save their friendship with Meg.

They smile at each other awkwardly, not sure how to bridge the silence. Then ANGELA spots one of the offending bridesmaids' shoes on a table, picks it up and exits into the other room.

LUCY watches her go, then childishly blows a raspberry and gives 'the finger' to the closed door. Then gradually… she seems to notice the audience. *The fourth wall slides away and the lighting state fades to be replaced by a spotlight, as we move into…*

SCENE TWO

Spotlight on LUCY. *She meets the audience's collective eyes, staring out at them a little defensively, then speaks.*

LUCY: Go on, look at me like that if you want, but I'm just trying to be a good friend here. It's not like I'm enjoying this… I can think of a lot more fun ways to spend a day, believe me—but real friends tell the truth. End of story. And it's all very well to hide behind niceness and lame excuses, but—Oh look, maybe that's not fair. Stuff it, I don't care—Angela's another one who's got this whole wedding thing way out of whack… [*Frustration tempered by amusement*] If you ask me—and I know you didn't—weddings are toxic. And I'll tell you why. Because they force decent people to lie. I mean, who can honestly say to another person, 'Yes, I know *for certain* that I'll forsake all others for the rest of my life?' [*She gives a little laugh: What a ridiculous notion.*] No-one, that's who. If you ask me, the vows should go, 'Right now I feel like forsaking all others, but let's consult again further down the track…' [*Amused for a moment, then she remembers the situation, and her anger returns.*] Jesus, if I saw James right now… Why ask Meg to marry him if he can't even keep his dick in his pants while they're *engaged*…? [*She meets the audience's collective eyes.*] Oh, yeah yeah, I know what you're thinking. Some couples *can* be happy forever. Well, they've won life's lottery. Half their luck. But the rest of us have to keep buying tickets…

And buying, and buying, and buying… Sometimes *I* feel like I'm running out of raffle books… Jesus, men have done terrible things to me, but I've treated them badly too. I've been unfaithful to a boyfriend once… [*thinking*] no, technically twice, and I'm not proud of that. But you know what else? I have *never* been unfaithful to a *friend.* Because friendship's too important to stuff around with. So, alright—I can wait till Kate rings, and I can cross all my fingers and toes that it isn't the same James, but if it *is*… I've never kept a friend in the dark—and wedding or no wedding, I'm not about to start.

Fade to black.

SCENE THREE

Lights up. MEG *has emerged fresh from her shower. She's wrapped in a fluffy white towel and carries a bottle of Chanel body lotion. Her hair is freshly blow-dried.*

ANGELA *is so eager to hide her tension that she shows a ridiculous amount of interest in* MEG*'s shower.*

ANGELA: Here she is! How was your shower? Hot enough for you?

MEG: Yeah, it was fine—

ANGELA: [*right over the top of her*] Good water pressure?

MEG: Huh—?

ANGELA: Was it good water pressure?

MEG: [*bemused*] Yeah, it was okay—

ANGELA: Did you manage alright without the loofah?

MEG: What? Yeah—

ANGELA: [*overlapping, pointing to her dry hair*] And you didn't wash your hair?

MEG: My shower's not really that interesting, Ange. You need to get out more.

> LUCY *re-enters, trying to mask her tension with joviality.*

LUCY: Hey, let's raid the mini-bar!

ANGELA: Great idea!

MEG: [*puzzled*] You don't drink.

ANGELA: Oh yeah. I forgot.

> MEG *gives her a funny look, then turns back to* LUCY.

MEG: Mum bought some champagne. It's in the fridge.

LUCY: [*opening the fridge*] Wooh. Four bottles.

> LUCY *busies herself getting out a champagne bottle, which she promptly drops.*

Ooops! Shit!

MEG: You're not getting nervous on me, are you Luce?

LUCY: [*a handy excuse*] I might be.

MEG: You big wuss-bag. If anyone should be getting jittery around here, it's *me*.

ANGELA: [*hastily, with significance*] Why? What's the matter? Are you worried about something?!

MEG *gives her a look: That was a strange reaction to a throwaway comment.*
MEG: No.
ANGELA can't take the tension anymore. She's got to get out of there.
ANGELA: I think *I'll* have a shower now.
LUCY: Great idea! See you later.
As ANGELA *heads for the bathroom, a barely perceptible look passes between she and* LUCY: *Don't even think about it.*
ANGELA *exits into the bathroom, closing the door.*
MEG *looks the tiniest bit puzzled, but* LUCY *distracts her with the champagne.*
Stand back, ladies and gentlemen, girls and boys—
MEG: [*overlapping*] Hang on a sec—can you put some of this on my back first?
She hands LUCY *the Chanel body lotion.*
LUCY: Sure.
MEG *turns away from* LUCY. LUCY *starts rubbing the body lotion into her back.*
MEG: Rub it all over, Luce.
As LUCY *rubs in the body lotion her face betrays her tension, but of course* MEG *can't see that.* LUCY*'s an impetuous person and it's a struggle not to blurt out the truth.*
The sound of a shower running comes from the bathroom.
LUCY: Hmm… This stuff reeks.
MEG: It'd want to, for one hundred and forty-eight bucks.
LUCY: One hundred and forty-eight bucks? I've had cars that cost less than that.
MEG: I know. I've had to push them. [*As* LUCY *starts rubbing it in*] Rache bought it for me—wasn't that sweet?
LUCY: [*impressed*] Yeah. *I* want a trainee.
MEG: [*laughing*] She's my partner now, or she will be soon… God, it's such a relief to know she'll keep things on track so I can just forget all about my clients and have a completely beautiful wedding and an R-rated honeymoon.

She laughs. LUCY *tries to laugh too, but* MEG *misinterprets her lack of enthusiasm.*

[*Light*] I know *you* think big weddings are lame, but you'll just have to humour me.

LUCY: I'm here, aren't I?

They laugh together.

MEG: I want everything to be perfect, Luce—the flowers, the food, the music, the lot. That's not too much to ask, is it? And don't even think about saying the 'Bridezilla' word.

They smile again. A short silence as LUCY *struggles internally, then:*

LUCY: [*feigned casual*] So listen, Bridezilla. How are you feeling about *after* the wedding? You know, the whole 'till death do you part' thing?

MEG: Great. Fantastic. Aren't the roses gorgeous?

LUCY: [*what?*] Hmm?

MEG *gestures towards the yellow roses on the table.*

MEG: James sent me those. The card said 'I will love you always'.

LUCY: Yeah, nice… [*She grins as a memory occurs.*] But you know what yellow roses remind me of—

MEG: [*overlapping, groaning*] I know, I know! Don't say it!

LUCY: Remember when you got me to send you those yellow roses with an anonymous card to make that bastard Jason jealous—?

MEG: Julian.

LUCY: What?

MEG: His name was Julian. And he didn't care less… [*A fond memory*] God, he was a dick. I adored him.

LUCY: Of course you did. Your taste in men sucked back then.

MEG: Ha! Look who's talking! What about—? [*Stopping as she has a sudden thought*] Oh, my God—David! Did David ring?!

LUCY: [*grinning*] We had dinner last night.

MEG: You *had dinner?! Now* she tells me. Why didn't you tell me?

LUCY: You were busy organising something—

MEG: So what happened? Where did you go?

LUCY: Vue de Monde.

MEG: Nice. Did he pick you up?

LUCY: Yep.

MEG *raises her eyebrows and whistles.*

MEG: Good sign. And what kind of car's he got?

LUCY: A blue one. I think it had two doors.

MEG: And what did you wear?

LUCY: The black halter-neck dress.

MEG: The one with the plunging back? I love that. And what about shoes?

LUCY: My killer boots.

MEG: The suede ones?

LUCY: [*nodding*] With the skinny heels.

MEG: Perfect! They make your legs look really long—not that you need that. And was it good…? [*Slightly tentative*] Did he talk about Claire…?

LUCY: Yeah.

MEG: Well? What did he say?

LUCY: He said he's over her—

MEG: [*interrupting*] Fantastic!

LUCY: Yeah, but who knows if it's true.

MEG: Well, what were his exact words?

LUCY: 'I'm over her.'

MEG: Yeah, but did he say I'm *over* her or I'm over *her*?

LUCY: See, this is the thing. I couldn't tell. And I tried to get him to say it again, but he didn't.

MEG: Well, could you talk to him? Was he witty or smart?

LUCY: [*nodding*] Witty *and* smart.

MEG: Interested in your life?

LUCY: Yeah, but they always sound interested in your life before they go to bed with you.

MEG: That's true.

Then LUCY *grins mischievously.*

LUCY: Mind you, he still sounded interested afterwards.

MEG *laughs and hits* LUCY *playfully.*

MEG: Ha! You did the deed?! You said you weren't going to do it on the first date anymore.

LUCY: I wasn't going to, but I couldn't help it. When he poured the wine his sleeves rode up, and he had arms like an AFL player—

MEG: [*overlapping*] I knew that, remember? I saw him in a singlet at Safeway that time—

LUCY: God, he's got seriously sexy arms... When he carried me into his room I melted—
MEG: He *carried you* into his room—?!
LUCY: [*nodding*] Yeah, and he picked me up like I weighed nothing.
MEG: Oh, my God... And how was the sex? Was it good?
LUCY: Amazing.
MEG: I knew it would be!
LUCY: As soon as he started kissing me I—
MEG: [*overlapping*] Good kisser?
LUCY: [*nodding*] Superb. He held my face in his hands—
MEG: Oh, my God... I *love* that!
LUCY: And that was it. I couldn't stop myself.
MEG: [*admiringly*] It's so great how you can't stop yourself. I've *always* been able to stop myself, no matter how advanced things are.
LUCY: [*grinning*] I wasn't stopping anything.
MEG: So are you going out again?
LUCY: [*shrugging*] He said he'd ring me on Wednesday.
MEG: Well, he'll ring you on Wednesday.
LUCY: No. If he was a *woman* and he said 'I'll ring you on Wednesday', he'd ring me on Wednesday, but he's a man so 'I'll ring you on Wednesday' means 'Maybe I'll ring you sometime if I feel like it'.
MEG: [*laughing*] Yeah, true.

>COLLEEN *re-enters with the place card box and an air of practised brightness.*

COLLEEN: Well, I've finished folding the place cards.
MEG: Thanks for doing that, Mum.
COLLEEN: [*holding one out*] See? You can see the whole sentence now.
MEG: Great. See, Lucy?

>LUCY *tries to look at the name card like it matters, but* COLLEEN *senses her lack of interest.*

LUCY: Yeah, great.

>COLLEEN *snatches the card from her and puts it back in its box with pursed lips.* LUCY *gestures to* MEG: *What did I do now?* MEG *jumps in to save things, as usual.*

MEG: We're going to open the champagne, Mum. Do you want a glass?
COLLEEN: Just a splash, Sweetheart. I won't officially break my diet till— [tomorrow.]

COLLEEN's *gaze suddenly falls onto the ribbons. She gasps in abject horror.*

Oh no! Oh no!

MEG: [*alarmed*] What?! What is it?!

COLLEEN: I forgot to bring the tape measure—!

MEG: What?

COLLEEN: [*picking up the ribbon*] For the ribbon—we need to cut it into one-metre lengths!

MEG: You said you were going to put it in your bag—

COLLEEN: I forgot! There were so many things to do—!

MEG: Remind me why it has to be exactly one metre, again?

COLLEEN: Because the ends of the pews are twenty-seven centimetres and it has to be long enough to go around them and make a big bow!

MEG: I'll ring Reception and see if they can send a tape measure up—

LUCY: But couldn't you just measure out the length you want—like this— [*grabbing the ribbon and demonstrating*] —and then do the same length again?

A small silence as MEG *and* COLLEEN *realise how incredibly simple it is.*

MEG: [*grinning*] Not just a pretty face.

COLLEEN: Yes, you're right. I suppose we could do that.

She makes a real effort to smile at LUCY *in a friendly fashion.*

Thank you, Lucy.

LUCY: That's okay. And, Colleen, I *am* sorry about the shoes—

COLLEEN: It's alright. I might have overreacted—slightly. We've had a lot of last-minute hiccups and I'd just found out that Naomi Bartlett's fellow is a vegetarian—

LUCY: [*overlapping, hopefully*] Naomi Bartlett's got a fellow?!

MEG: No. She's bringing some guy she met at Pilates.

LUCY: [*deflated*] Oh.

COLLEEN: And Meg's Great Uncle Reg isn't invited. But anyway, we won't get into that...

The shower is heard been turned off.

The important thing is that we're all here together, celebrating Meg's special day.

MEG: Oh, Mum… let's just get into that champers, eh?
LUCY: Stand back!

    LUCY *pops the cork. They make ad lib reactions.*

MEG: Wooh! Quick, quick! It's all fizzy! [*etc.*]

    COLLEEN *and* MEG *grab champagne glasses to catch the bubbles. Ad lib laughter.*

    As LUCY *pours the champagne into the glasses,* ANGELA *re-enters from the bathroom wearing a silky nightie. She looks fresh and cleansed, and she's had time to reconstruct her air of calm. Her wet hair is wrapped in a towel.*

COLLEEN: Oh, Angela, you're just in time for a glass of champagne.
MEG: She doesn't drink, Mum.
COLLEEN: Oh, of course. I knew that.
MEG: There's lemonade and orange juice in the fridge, Ange.
ANGELA: Actually, I'm more hungry than thirsty. Is anyone else hungry?
LUCY: Yeah, I'm starving.
COLLEEN: [*nodding*] I'm a bit hungry.
MEG: Oh, I'm sorry. I didn't even think about dinner.
COLLEEN: Well, you've had a lot of other things on your mind, Sweetheart.

    LUCY*'s mobile phone starts ringing.*

    LUCY *and* ANGELA *dart a startled look at one another.*

LUCY: Oooh! Oh, that's my mobile!
ANGELA: [*over her, startled*] That's your phone!

    As LUCY *gets her mobile out of her bag,* MEG *shakes her head in bemusement.*

MEG: Your nerves are shot to pieces, Luce. [*Turning to* ANGELA] Hey, why don't we get a pizza?
ANGELA: [*pre-occupied by* LUCY*'s phone call*] What?
LUCY: [*into her phone*] Hello?
MEG: [*to* ANGELA] Let's see if room service does a pizza.
ANGELA: [*distracted*] Yeah, pizza would be good.

    As MEG *grabs the room service menu:*

LUCY: [*into the phone*] Oh. No. Everything's fine. No thank you. I'm fine. Goodbye.

She hangs up. They're all staring at her, especially ANGELA.

It was Telstra. [*In an Indian accent*] Am I happy with my plan?

MEG: God. How rude to ring on a Friday night. Is pizza okay with you, Mum?

COLLEEN: Fine. As long as it's low-fat cheese.

ANGELA: But no anchovies.

The telephone starts to ring.

LUCY *and* ANGELA *jump, then quickly realise it's not* LUCY*'s mobile.*

COLLEEN: I'll get that.

She walks over to the phone and picks it up. Meanwhile, ANGELA *is a nervous wreck.*

ANGELA: Do you know what? I think I *will* have a glass of champagne.

MEG: [*surprised*] Are you sure, Ange?

ANGELA: Yeah, it's a special occasion.

She pours herself a glass of champagne, her hand shaking a little. Meanwhile…

COLLEEN: [*into the phone*] Hello? Oh, hello Bill. [*Mouthing to* MEG] It's Dad.

MEG: [*looking at the menu*] Yeah, there's a couple of pizzas.

LUCY: [*looking at the menu*] Have any of them got pancetta?

COLLEEN: [*gasping into the phone*] They did *what?!* Well, that's just marvellous! [*To the girls, her hand over the receiver*] They delivered the bridal registry gifts to Pakenham Upper!

MEG: What?!

COLLEEN: Did you fix it? Now are you sure it's sorted out? Alright…

She gestures to MEG: *It's alright. Relieved,* MEG *turns her attention to the pizzas. With* ANGELA *and* LUCY *she makes the decision: pancetta, figs and goat's cheese. And garlic bread. Meanwhile…*

'Bye, then… Oh—Oh, Bill—you'll have to be here by eight thirty in the morning to pick up the place cards and ribbon—and I want Jenny to tie the bows because you can't tie a bow to save yourself. Oh, and my spare pair of pantyhose are on top of the dryer. Thanks, 'bye.

She hangs up and turns to the young women, enjoying the latest drama.

Well, what a shemozzle!

MEG: What happened? Is it fixed?
COLLEEN: It's alright. Your father's sorted it out. But apparently there are two James Davises getting married tomorrow, and one of them lives in Pakenham Upper.

    ANGELA *gives* LUCY *an excited look. Vindication.*

ANGELA: Two James Davises?
COLLEEN: Yes, apparently.
ANGELA: [*for* LUCY*'s benefit*] *Two* men called James Davis are getting married tomorrow?
COLLEEN: [*nodding*] That's what Bill said.
LUCY: Two separate weddings with two James Davises?
COLLEEN: [*getting impatient*] Yes!
LUCY: [*blurting to* ANGELA, *pleased*] Well, that changes everything.
ANGELA: [*warning*] Lucy—
MEG: [*interrupting*] What do you mean, that changes everything?
LUCY: I don't know what I mean. [*Turning to* ANGELA] What do I mean?
ANGELA: I don't know.

    Fade to black.

SCENE FOUR

Spotlight on ANGELA. *She stands in her bathrobe, towelling her hair dry as she talks directly to the audience.*

ANGELA: I like Lucy, I really do, but she makes me feel like I'm the kind of person who buys all their clothes at Katies. I've bought maybe two skirts and one top there in twenty years. And so what if I bought *everything* there? What would it matter? And why am I talking about Katies, anyway…? [*She sighs, then composes herself.*] Oh, I don't know… How can I explain a lifelong commitment to someone who doesn't want to understand? What could I say to her? That I look at John and I see my home? It sounds too cutesie for words, but it's true. I've always felt like that. Ever since we met. I was only seventeen, and he was my first ever boyfriend—well, except for Darren O'Brien, but that doesn't really count, because he only touched my boobs twice, and I cried afterwards. [*Getting a bit sidetracked*] I can't remember why I cried. Maybe I had my period? No, that's right, yeah—he pinched my nipples, and it really hurt. Anyway, I married the only guy I'd ever had sex with. Can you imagine what Lucy would think about that? Well, I *know* what she thinks. She thinks I'm a nerdy mum from the suburbs who's had an easy ride. And she thinks I don't understand what's going on with James and Meg—but *she's wrong...*

[*Vulnerable*] The thing is, James is a nice man... And nice people make mistakes sometimes. He's probably torturing himself about it, and isn't that punishment enough? And he adores Meg. I can see it in his eyes. And as for her, well, I haven't seen her this happy since we won the Wham! competition when we were nine. George Michael kissed her, and she got to hold Andrew Ridgeley's hand, and she was so-o-o-o excited... Oh, except Mrs Bacon took some photos and they didn't turn out. That was such a bummer. [*She stops. Getting back to the point*] Anyway, the point is, Meg's ecstatic. And Lucy expects me to just just turn around and destroy that for her, without knowing any of the facts? I won't do it. [*A beat or two.*] It's all very well for Lucy to be so self-righteous, but what's *she* got to lose? It's not *her* future she's playing with. And besides, friendship's not about gratifying your own ego, it's about doing what's best for your friend. And James is the best thing that's ever happened to Meg. I still believe that. And I know that men... and women, too... do things that they regret sometimes. But if the commitment's there, a couple can come out on the other side, with their relationship stronger and deeper than ever... [*Beat.*] I don't want to be responsible for Meg missing out on that.

Fade to black.

SCENE FIVE

It's about two hours later.

Empty room service plates lie around, one with a half-eaten gourmet pizza plus several empty and/or half-empty bottles of champagne.

COLLEEN *sits at the table, wearing a dressing-gown. She's measuring out the silver ribbon and cutting it into appropriate lengths. She's concentrating madly, so she's not really listening to* LUCY *and* MEG.

LUCY *and* MEG *sit on* MEG*'s bed, wearing their pyjamas. They're both loosened up by alcohol.* MEG *is chirpy as she paints her toenails, while*

LUCY *flips through* Grazia. LUCY *is more relaxed now that she knows there are two James Davises, but she still keeps glancing at a clock. It's about 9.50 p.m.*

MEG: Hey, I've got a good one, Luce—
LUCY: Okay, hit me with it.
MEG: If Brad Pitt and Johnny Depp were both in town on the same night, and they both wanted to see you, but you could only see one—which one would you see?
LUCY: [*grinning*] Define 'see'.

> MEG *grins back and gestures towards* COLLEEN, *who is concentrating on the ribbons: Don't get too graphic with Mum in the room.*

[*Laughing*] Johnny. Definitely.
MEG: [*surprised*] You wouldn't do it with Brad?
LUCY: [*shaking her head*] Nah. Johnny's much sexier.
MEG: [*dubiously*] You reckon?
LUCY: [*fervently*] God, yeah. He's all messy and mysterious.
MEG: I can kind of see that… but he's slept with supermodels. I'd be too self-conscious.
LUCY: Meg. Brad's slept with *Angelina*.
MEG: [*light*] She doesn't exist in this scenario. And neither do the fifteen kids.
LUCY: [*shaking her head*] I'd still do it with Johnny.
MEG: But Brad's so gorgeous.
LUCY: Exactly. You really want to have sex with a guy who's physically perfect?
MEG: Yeah, I'm weird like that.

> *The women share a girlie chuckle, then:*

Anyway, I can't do it with either of them. I'm an old married woman now, almost.

> LUCY *is brought back to reality with a thud.*

LUCY: What's the time?
MEG: Ten to ten. Hey, Mum—
COLLEEN: Thirty-five, thirty-six, thirty-seven… Hmm?
MEG: If Harrison Ford and… Matt Preston were both in town on the same night and—

COLLEEN: [*interrupting*] Twenty-nine!
MEG: What?
COLLEEN: There's only enough ribbon here for twenty-nine pews!
MEG: But you said you were going to get enough for thirty!
COLLEEN: I did, Meg. I asked for thirty metres. They must've measured it wrong—
LUCY: [*overlapping*] But you're not doing it in one-metre lengths. You haven't got the tape measure, remember? So you don't know the exact length of the pieces.
COLLEEN: [*to* MEG] See? I *knew* I should've borrowed a tape measure! Now what are we going to do?
MEG: Well, we'll just have to put bows on twenty-nine pews—
COLLEEN: We can't have an *uneven* number of bows!
MEG: Well then, we can put the bows on twenty-eight pews—
COLLEEN: [*overlapping*] No! I've worked it out in my head, Meg, and the bride's side will take up sixteen pews!
LUCY: Well, how many pews will James' side take up?
COLLEEN: About ten.
LUCY: Then you only need twenty-six ribbons, don't you?
COLLEEN: No. It's bad manners to have less ribbons on the groom's side.
LUCY: Then how about not having any ribbons?
COLLEEN: [*snapping sharply*] Don't be ridiculous!
MEG: Mum, Lucy's just trying to help. We'll just have to make do with twenty-nine ribbons—
COLLEEN: But it's an *uneven* number—
MEG: No-one will notice—
COLLEEN: Jan Grainger will notice, I promise you.
LUCY: [*can't help herself*] Oh, for God's sake! Does this matter?!
MEG: Lucy… She didn't mean it, Mum.
COLLEEN: Oh, yes she did. I'm sorry if this wedding doesn't matter to *you*, Lucy, but it matters a lot to me, and a lot to Meg.
LUCY: I know. I'm sorry. I just don't think you should waste so much energy on ribbons. There must be more important things to worry about.

But the sub-text is lost on MEG *and* COLLEEN.

COLLEEN: I just want Meg to have a nice day. Is that such a crime?

MEG *moves over to her mother and puts her arm around her shoulders.*

MEG: Of course not, Mum. If you're still worried about the ribbon in the morning, we can get Dad to come a bit earlier and stop off at Spotlight on his way to the church. Or Jenny could buy it—
COLLEEN: That's true. But how will she know what width to get?
MEG: She could come here and pick up the ribbons first. And they'll cut it for her at Spotlight.
COLLEEN: [*appeased*] Oh, alright, that makes sense.

> LUCY *takes another sip of her champagne, holding herself back, as the bathroom door opens and* ANGELA *emerges.*

ANGELA: I think I'm a bit drunk...

> *She flops down onto the bed like a rag doll.* MEG *and* COLLEEN *exchange worried looks.*

MEG: Are you okay?
ANGELA: Yeah... I'm fine...
COLLEEN: Are you sure, Angela?
ANGELA: [*quickly sitting up*] Yeah, I'm fine, Mrs Bacon.
COLLEEN: Alright then. Well, I'm off to bed. You should get to sleep soon too, Sweetheart.
MEG: I will, Mum. I just have to finish my toenails.
COLLEEN: Angela, you're in with me, aren't you?
ANGELA: Yes, Mrs Bacon. I'll be in... some time after ten thirty.

> LUCY *and* ANGELA *exchange a look as* COLLEEN *kisses* MEG *on the cheek.*

COLLEEN: Well, I'll see you on your special day...
MEG: 'Night, Mum... Sleep well...
LUCY/ANGELA: Goodnight, Colleen / Mrs Bacon. [*etc.*]

> *A drunk* ANGELA *throws her arms around* COLLEEN *in an overly-enthusiastic hug. It takes* COLLEEN *a while to extricate herself.*

COLLEEN: You always were an affectionate child... Goodnight. Don't keep Meg up too late.
ANGELA: We won't.

> COLLEEN *exits.*

LUCY: Sorry about upsetting her, Meg—
MEG: Forget it, Luce. I've had fifteen years to get used to you two. [*Playfully pushing her off the bed*] Get off, go on...

As LUCY *gets off the bed,* MEG *climbs back on and resumes painting her toenails. In the meantime,* LUCY *assembles the folding bed.*

Hey, I've got another one: Ange—would you rather be a topless waitress or a parking officer?

ANGELA *grimaces at the horrific options.*

ANGELA: Oh, yuk… They're both horrible… Can you lie about your job?
MEG: No, you have to go to parties and tell the whole truth.
LUCY: Shit. I'd be a topless waitress. [*Her mobile phone rings.*] Ohh! That's my mobile again—

LUCY *and* ANGELA *exchange a look as* LUCY *grabs her phone: The moment of truth.*

MEG: At ten o'clock on a Friday night? Why don't you turn it off?
LUCY: [*into her phone*] Hello?
MEG: Who's going to ring someone at ten o'clock on a Friday?

ANGELA *shrugs in what she hopes is a casual manner.*

LUCY: [*into the phone*] No, you've got the wrong number. Yeah, 'bye.

She hangs up. She and ANGELA *exchange a look: The tension is killing them.*

MEG: Just turn it off, Luce—
ANGELA: [*frazzled*] Let's open another bottle!

She flops down like a rag doll again.

Fade to black.

SCENE SIX

Spotlight on COLLEEN. *She wears a floral nightie and carries a toiletries bag. Savouring a delicious feeling of anticipation, she addresses the audience directly.*

COLLEEN: You know, I opened a wedding account for Meg two weeks after she was born. It's added up to quite a nice amount now, much more than I'd ever thought, but then, we weren't expecting to wait thirty-three years… Oh, it did look like she was going to marry Paul when she was in her late twenties, but he got cold feet. It broke her heart I think, and she didn't meet James till quite a while later. And in the meantime the questions from our friends started. 'So your Meg's still single then?' And I'd smile and say, 'Oh, she's a career girl!' But I could see they were feeling sorry for me and wondering where me and Bill had gone wrong. Honestly, it was so silly. And then they all started having grandchildren, and do you think we ever heard the end of that? I swear, if I'd had to look at one more baby photo… [*She allows herself a smug smile.*] But anyway, it's all worked out for the best now, because Meg's got James—and he's a lawyer. And he owns a house and an inner-city apartment—oh, not that that matters of course, but I have to say he's a lot more successful than any of Jan Grainger's sons-in-law. And so is Meg, now I come to think of it! [*She ponders that for a pleasing moment.*] I've spent months planning every detail for tomorrow—because every girl deserves a beautiful wedding. She should be able to show off those photos forever and say, 'That was the happiest day of my life and everything was perfect'. [*Suddenly tight*] Goodness knows you don't want people saying 'Is that a coffin in the corner?' like they say when they look at my wedding photos. But yes, there's a coffin behind me and Bill when we're signing the register. It looks like I'm balancing it on my left shoulder. 'Part bride, part pallbearer' some wag once said, and they thought it was funny, but it wasn't. [*The façade crumbling further*] It was supposed to be my special day, but there were grieving relatives weeping on the front steps so we had to have our photos taken round the back of the church. We didn't want to upset them with our happiness—not that I was happy—because nothing was the way I wanted it—and I'm not just talking about the funeral—I didn't have any say in anything— But anyway, that was a long time ago, and it's Meg's turn now. And her wedding's going to be perfect—

[*Losing it again*] Because my mother—God rest her soul, is gone—so she can't hijack Meg's wedding like she did mine!

Fade to black.

SCENE SEVEN

It's about 10.15 now. More alcohol has been consumed. LUCY, ANGELA *and* MEG *are lazing around in their PJs, indulging in some fun 'girl talk'. As* LUCY *tells an anecdote,* ANGELA *and* MEG *listen intently.* ANGELA *is a little tipsier than the other two.*

LUCY: ... Anyway, he was texting her almost every day and asking her out to the movies and stuff, so finally Suse had to say to him, 'Look—I like you, but I don't think I like you, you know...'
MEG/ANGELA: [*overlapping, in unison*] Like *that.*
LUCY: Yeah. 'Cause she was trying to be fair—
MEG: [*nodding*] Like you do—
LUCY: Yeah. And *he* said, 'Well, I *was* hoping for more, but I really appreciate your honesty. And if friendship's all you can offer, I'd love to be your friend.'
ANGELA: Well, that's really nice, isn't it—?
LUCY: [*overlapping*] Yeah it was, but then two days later—are you listening—*forty-eight hours later*—Suse thought, 'Well, friendship's a two-way street, I guess *I* should call *him*'—so she rings him—and he tells her that he's really sorry to hurt her, but he just can't give her what she wants.

    ANGELA *and* MEG *laugh, gasp and shake their heads in a Typical Man gesture.*

ANGELA: Why did he do that?
LUCY: Who the hell knows?
ANGELA: And what did he think she wanted anyway?
LUCY: [*grinning*] To marry him of course.
ANGELA: But she was the one who said she didn't— [feel that way.]
LUCY: [*overlapping*] I know! But he's a man so that's not what he heard.
ANGELA: They're amazing, aren't they?
LUCY: [*nodding*] Awe-inspiring.

    Silence for a moment, then...

MEG: Imagine if you could harness the energy of the male ego and use it for good instead of evil? Pass me the champers, Luce...
ANGELA: More for me too.
MEG: Are you sure, Ange?
ANGELA: [*overlapping, slightly sozzled*] You know what *I* don't get about men? Why so many of them want to be with women who, well... you know... aren't quite as intelligent as—
LUCY: [*overlapping*] Women who are *dumb*, Angela. Tell it like it is. A lot of guys want to be with dumb chicks.

MEG: Can you imagine anything more boring than having some dumb but good-looking guy at home, who cooked your meals and kept the house tidy and agreed with everything you said?

They stop and think about this for a moment.

Actually, that sounds quite appealing…
LUCY: I could handle it for a while.
ANGELA: I don't know. I don't think I could have sex with a dumb guy…
LUCY: I could. I can. I have.
ANGELA: Really? How many?
LUCY: Times, or dumb guys?
ANGELA: Dumb guys.
LUCY: Just the one. A guy called Nick.
MEG: [*clearing her throat*] Hhhhm… Craig.
LUCY: Just the two.
ANGELA: And was it good?
LUCY: It was great until he opened his mouth. To *talk*.

LUCY *and* MEG *laugh together.*

ANGELA: See? You *couldn't* be with a dumb guy. And we should be fair to men I suppose—
MEG: [*overlapping, jokingly*] Oh, why should we? That's no fun.
ANGELA: I mean, there are lots of men out there who don't want to be with dumb women either. Every brainy married woman has to be married to someone.
LUCY: Yeah, but hear that pivotal word 'married'? All the good men are taken.
MEG: Not necessarily. What about David?
LUCY: Yeah. Well. We'll see.
ANGELA: Who's David?
MEG: Lucy had a hot date last night.
ANGELA: Really?! Was it good? Is he nice?
LUCY: He's gorgeous, but he's *just* broken up with his girlfriend.
ANGELA: Well, Meg always says that's the best time to get them.
LUCY: [*grinning*] Yes, I'm familiar with that theory—
MEG: [*overlapping*] It's true. The good ones are only single for a week at a time, and you have to give them a few days to grieve, so that leaves you with a three-day window of opportunity, and that's when you have to pounce.

ANGELA: This guy sounds perfect, then.
LUCY: Yeah, but I think he's still hung-up on Claire.
MEG: No he's not. [*Turning to* ANGELA] He told Lucy he's over her. Those were his exact words: 'I'm over her'.
ANGELA: But did he say 'I'm *over* her' or 'I'm over *her*'?
LUCY: See this is the thing. I couldn't tell.
> *They all silently ponder this for a beat or two, then...*

Look, it's *my* fault I can't find the right guy. I shouldn't have stuffed around so much in my twenties… It's like I was in this awsome shoe shop, but I kept picking pairs that gave me blisters—and by the time I realised what shoes would fit, they didn't have any left in my size.
> LUCY *is amused by her own analogy, as are* MEG *and* ANGELA.

MEG: Oh, thank you, God… I don't want to rub it in, Luce, but this just makes me want to run right over to James' place and marry him tonight. God, I'm so glad I'll never have to go on another date.
> *This brings* ANGELA *and* LUCY *back to reality a bit. They exchange a worried look.*

LUCY: What's the time?
MEG: Twenty past ten. I should cleanse and tone.
> MEG *gets to her feet as Lucy's mobile starts ringing again.*

LUCY/ANGELA: [*startled*] Aaagh!
MEG: [*laughing*] Look at you two—nerves of steel. I thought you were going to turn that thing off…
> *As* LUCY *walks over to pick up her phone,* MEG *heads for the bathroom.*

[*Lightly*] Who calls someone at twenty past ten on a Friday…?
LUCY: [*into her phone*] Hello? Oh, hi Kate.
MEG: Kate? From work…?
> MEG *waves, mouths the words: Say hi from me, then exits into the bathroom.*

LUCY: [*into the phone*] Oh, I'm just sitting here with Meg… and Angela… yeah… great, no, we had a pizza…
> MEG *exits into the bathroom, closing the door behind her.*

[*Lowering her voice*] Okay—She's in the bathroom. Yeah... yeah? Davis. [*Turning to* ANGELA] It's James Davis!
ANGELA: But there are *two!*
LUCY: [*snapping at her*] I know that! [*Into the phone*] Does he live at Pakenham Upper? Well, ask your friend to ask her. Shit!
ANGELA: What? What?

> ANGELA's *tapping* LUCY *on the shoulder to get her attention.* LUCY's *incredibly irritated. She slaps* ANGELA's *hand away as she continues with the phone call.*

LUCY: [*into the phone*] Is she coming back? Well, call me if she does. Thanks Kate. 'Bye. [*She hangs up, and turns to* ANGELA.] Davis. That's all she knows. We'll have to ring the guy in Pakenham Upper—What's that number where they connect you direct?
ANGELA: One-two-four-five-six—
LUCY: [*starting to press the numbers*] One-two-four-five—
ANGELA: [*interrupting*] But it's really expensive.
LUCY: I don't care! [*Into the phone*] Oh hi—yes, James Davis, in Pakenham Upper— [*Crossing her fingers*] Thanks—Yes! They're connecting me—
ANGELA: What are you going to say?
LUCY: Fucked if I know. It's ringing! Oh, it's a machine—He sounds really old—hold on— [*She listens.*] Shit, oh... God...

> *She looks like she doesn't know whether to laugh or cry.*

ANGELA: What?!
LUCY: [*hanging up*] He's President of the Pakenham Seniors Club.
ANGELA: [*doesn't know whether to laugh or cry either*] Oh...

> *They look at each other in silence for a moment, the full implications dawning, then...*

LUCY: Well, Naomi wouldn't be fucking a grandad. When Meg comes out of the bathroom we'll just have to tell her.
ANGELA: No! I still say we don't.
LUCY: Oh, what?! But it's *him!*
ANGELA: Yeah, but don't forget Kate said it's over now—
LUCY: So? What's that got to do with— [anything?!]
ANGELA: [*interrupting*] And he's made Meg happy. You can't deny that.
LUCY: Yeah, but only because she doesn't— [know about this.]

ANGELA: [*interrupting*] And *you* thought he was good for her too. You *told me* that—!
LUCY: Yeah, but I didn't know what he was doing—
ANGELA: But he's still the same person you liked, Lucy.
LUCY: Bullshit!
ANGELA: I don't think we should tell her.

> LUCY *looks at her like she's a complete moron.*

LUCY: *What* is your problem?
ANGELA: [*firmly*] It's a bad idea.
LUCY: How can you *say* that?

> ANGELA *looks* LUCY *square in the eye. When she speaks again her tone is even firmer.*

ANGELA: Look, I know Meg. You'll just have to trust me.

> LUCY *would like to hit her over the head with a cricket bat, but instead she tries to reason with her.*

LUCY: Angela, it's nice that you don't want to hurt her, and if I thought that Meg and James could have what you and... [*searching for* ANGELA*'s husband's name*] you and...
ANGELA: [*tersely*] John.
LUCY: You and John have, I wouldn't want to either. But there aren't many relationships as perfect as yours—
ANGELA: [*overlapping, irritated*] Ours isn't perfect—
LUCY: Okay, not perfect, but it's obviously been pretty smooth sailing compared to other people's—
ANGELA: Not always. We've had our ups and downs—
LUCY: Well, yeah, but something like this would never be an issue with you guys—
ANGELA: [*hissing*] For God's sake, Lucy. *I've* had an affair!
LUCY: *What?!*
ANGELA: [*eyes darting towards the bathroom*] I've had an affair.
LUCY: [*stunned*] *You've* had an affair?
ANGELA: [*nodding, low*] It was last year, and I didn't think I'd ever—
LUCY: [*interrupting*] Was he a friend of John's?
ANGELA: What? No! No way, as if I'd— Look, I went to a teacher's conference and I met this man and I just, I never expected to do anything like that, but I'd only ever been with John and... it happened.

LUCY: *You've* had an affair?
ANGELA: Yes. Maybe I'm not quite as boring as you thought.
LUCY: I never said you were boring—
ANGELA: [*overlapping*] Anyway—it went on for a couple of months, but all it did was make me realise how lucky I am to have John, and I felt incredibly guilty, so I told him…
LUCY: You told him?

> ANGELA *nods.*

Well, there you go—
ANGELA: [*shaking her head*] If I had my time again, I wouldn't tell him—well, first of all I wouldn't *do it*—but if I did, I wouldn't tell him. It was horrible, Lucy. I nearly lost him. We're only just back on track now. And if I hadn't told him, we wouldn't have gone through any of it.

> LUCY *is still stunned by this information.*

LUCY: And did Meg know about this?
ANGELA: Yes.
LUCY: Well, what did she say—?
ANGELA: She told me not to tell him.

> *This hangs in the air for a moment. But* LUCY*'s compulsive honesty propels her forward.*

LUCY: Yeah, alright—but everyone knows it's different when it's *you*. I still think *she'd* want to know.
ANGELA: I'm not sure she would.
LUCY: But what if she found out in six months and knew that we knew and didn't tell her? How would we feel then?
ANGELA: And if we *do* tell her, she might call off her wedding and miss out on fifty fantastic years with James. For all we know he'll never do it again.
LUCY: But I can't live with myself if I don't tell her the truth.
ANGELA: But maybe *she* couldn't live with herself if you did.

> *The bathroom door opens and* MEG *re-emerges, rubbing moisturiser into her face.*

MEG: What did Kate want?

> ANGELA *jumps in quickly before* LUCY *can answer.*

ANGELA: She's going to work tomorrow! She needs one of Lucy's files for research.

MEG: Oh…

> MEG *plonks herself onto the bed.* ANGELA *and* LUCY *look awkward: What should they do?*

> [*Grinning*] What are you standing there like idiots for? Sit down.

> *She pats the bed beside her, but* LUCY *and* ANGELA *sit at the table in a single, swift, self-conscious movement.* MEG *gives them an odd look, then starts playing with an empty champagne bottle, spinning it absent-mindedly.*

> Hey, you know how they reckon wine's good for you now, for your heart?

LUCY: Well, *red* wine is.

MEG: Oh, is it only *red* wine?

LUCY: Yeah.

MEG: Bummer. I was going to say, 'Do you reckon it's the same for champagne?'

LUCY: Not in these copious quantities.

> MEG *suddenly looks down at the bottle she's been absent-mindedly spinning.*

MEG: Hey, let's play Truth or Dare!

ANGELA: What?

MEG: Come on, it'll be fun! We'll spin the bottle. Who wants to go first?

LUCY: Truth or Dare?

MEG: Yeah. Come on—

> *A barely perceptible look between* LUCY *and* ANGELA*: This could be a way to work out whether* MEG *would want to know about James. A silent agreement.*

ANGELA: Okay. Let's do it.

LUCY: [*overlapping*] Yeah, okay, let's.

MEG: [*grinning*] Great.

> *They move over to join her on the bed as* MEG *grabs the bottle, preparing to spin…*

ANGELA: I haven't played Truth or Dare since I was sixteen. [*Reminding* MEG] You were there, remember? At Astrid's place. I had to kiss—

> MEG *joins in. They say it in unison:*

ANGELA/MEG: Errr—Robert McDougall…!
MEG: Uggghh… with the green teeth. Gross. And he stuck his tongue in and twirled it around, remember—?
ANGELA: Errggh… stop it… I've spent seventeen years trying to forget.
MEG: [*laughing*] I'll go first—
LUCY: Go for it, Meg.

> MEG *spins the bottle and it lands on* ANGELA.

MEG: Ha! Ange!
ANGELA: Oh, no…
LUCY: Make it a juicy one.
MEG: Okay, truth or dare?
ANGELA: [*grimacing*] Truth.
MEG: Okay, let's see… [*Taking a few beats to think of a question*] Oh, I know— If John wanted to wear your lingerie, would you let him?
ANGELA: Depends. Do *I* want to wear it that day?

> MEG *and* LUCY *laugh in surprise at her blasé answer.*

MEG: Ange!
LUCY: You'd let him?
ANGELA: Anything except my Calvin Klein camisole. It's cream, and that's not a good colour for his complexion. My turn—

> *She starts spinning the bottle. The others are staring at her. She catches the look.*

[*Laughing*] *I'm* allowed to crack jokes too.

> *The bottle stops, pointing to* LUCY.

Lucy! Okay, truth or dare—?
LUCY: [*subtext*] You know me. Truth every time.
ANGELA: Alright, alright— Okay, let me think—okay—where's the strangest place you've ever had sex?
LUCY: At the City Baths. While people were doing laps all around us.
ANGELA: [*gasping*] You didn't?!
LUCY: I did. In the medium lane.
MEG: With Michael?
LUCY: Yeah.
MEG: [*laughing*] That'd be right.
ANGELA: [*impressed*] You could've been arrested, Lucy.

LUCY: Yeah, but we weren't. My turn.

She grabs the bottle and blatantly moves it so it's pointing towards MEG.

Meg. You.

MEG: That was rigged! You didn't spin it!

LUCY: [*lying brazenly*] Yes I did. Truth or dare?

MEG: [*to* ANGELA] Did you see that? She rigged it.

LUCY: Come on—truth or dare?

MEG: Truth.

A barely perceptible look passes between LUCY *and* ANGELA.

LUCY: Okay— Truth: If James was having an affair—right now, with twelve hours to go till the wedding—would you want to know?

Silence hangs in the air for a moment. ANGELA *can hardly bear to look at* MEG. *They're both desperate to hear her answer.*

MEG: [*after a beat*] Dare.

LUCY/ANGELA: What?

MEG: I'll take the dare.

LUCY: Don't you want to answer the question?

MEG: I'll take the dare.

LUCY: You could take the dare and answer the question.

MEG: That's not the game, Luce.

ANGELA: God knows what dare she'll give you though, Meg. If I was you I'd stick with the truth.

MEG: I said I'm taking the dare, okay?

LUCY: You're sure you don't want to take the truth?

MEG: Why? Can't you think of a good dare?

LUCY: [*thwarted*] Of course I can. Alright… I dare you to ring room service and ask for a penis butter sandwich.

MEG *and* ANGELA *guffaw, etc.*

MEG: Oh, what?!

LUCY: You heard me. Ask them to send up a penis butter sandwich.

MEG: [*laughing*] I can't do that.

LUCY: Then answer the question.

MEG: No, I mean, I *can* do it, but it's so childish!

LUCY: Oh, derrr… I thought that was the whole point.

MEG: Here. Give me the phone— [*Grabbing the hotel phone, and looking at the numbers*] This is *so* embarrassing. What number's Room Service?
ANGELA: It's not too late to pick the truth.
MEG: It's okay. I'll do the stupid dare.

> *In spite of themselves,* ANGELA *and* LUCY *can't help giggling as* MEG *dials the number.*

LUCY: They're going to know what room this is, you know. As soon as they pick it up—
ANGELA: [*overlapping*] Yeah, the number lights up—
MEG: [*overlapping*] Sssssh! [*Embarrassed, giggling, etc. Into the phone*] Oh, hello. Umm… it's *Lucy Dean* from Room 304 here…
LUCY: [*calling into the phone*] No, it's Meg Bacon!
MEG: [*pushing her away, back on the phone*] Umm… we were wondering if we could get some… umm… room service… Yeah, we'd like a round of, ah… of, umm… of… penis butter sandwiches—

> ANGELA *and* LUCY *fall about laughing.*

[*Giggling*] Yeah, that's right… penis butter… Oh, you don't have that—?
LUCY: Then ask if they've got some vaginamite!

> MEG *bursts into guffaws of laughter and hangs up the phone. They're all in fits of giggles.*

MEG: Vaginamite?!
ANGELA: What did they say—?
MEG: [*laughing*] He was so polite, the poor thing—
LUCY: Did he laugh?
MEG: No! I've never felt like such a dickhead. I'm going to get you for this—

> MEG *takes the bottle and blatantly moves it so it's pointing at* LUCY.

Truth or Dare?
LUCY: [*another look to* ANGELA] Truth.
MEG: I want you to take the dare.
LUCY: No. I'm taking the truth.
MEG: Take the dare, you scumbag.
LUCY: No. Unlike *some people,* I'm not afraid of the truth.
ANGELA: It's Meg's right not to pick the truth, Lucy.

But the sub-text of the argument is lost on MEG, *who is busy thinking of a question.*

MEG: God, I can't think of a single question that would embarrass *you*...
ANGELA: I've got one.
LUCY: Okay. What is it?
ANGELA: Truth: Have you ever had sex with a woman?
LUCY: [*grinning*] Define sex.
MEG: [*laughingly shocked*] Lucy!
ANGELA: [*embarrassed*] Well, sex... you know. Penetration.
LUCY: [*grinning*] Hmmm... let me think...
MEG: [*laughing*] No way! She would've told me if she'd—
LUCY: [*interrupting*] Yes.
MEG: What?!

Shock waves. LUCY *smiles, enjoying the reaction.*

You haven't had sex with a woman.
LUCY: Yes, I have.
MEG: No, you haven't.
LUCY: Meg. I picked the *truth*.
ANGELA: [*impressed*] You really have? How many times?
LUCY: Twice—but both on the same night, so that probably counts as once.

ANGELA *is shocked but impressed. Meanwhile,* MEG *is starting to look a little miffed.*

MEG: Who with?
LUCY: [*with the slightest hint of discomfort*] Just someone.
MEG: What do you mean, just *someone*?
LUCY: Just a woman.
ANGELA: [*blurting*] And what did you do?

LUCY *gives her a look. She's embarrassed.*

I mean, you know... *how* exactly...?
LUCY: [*joking*] Want me to show you?

She pretends she's going to pounce on ANGELA. ANGELA *squeals with laughter.*

ANGELA: No...! Lucy...!

But MEG *isn't laughing. She's still taken aback.*

MEG: When did this happen?
LUCY: After that party at Ben's place.
MEG: Ben's birthday party? Last year?
LUCY: [*nodding, slightly awkward*] Yeah.
ANGELA: And what was it like? Was it good?
LUCY: It was okay, but I like blokes better.
MEG: I can't believe you didn't tell me. Why didn't you tell me?
LUCY: [*shrugging*] I don't know. Why? You're not upset?
MEG: Well, it's just a bit weird that something like this happened months ago and I didn't even know about it.
LUCY: But it was such a non-event, I didn't think to—
MEG: [*interrupting*] A what—? Lucy, you had sex with a *woman*. That's an *event*.
LUCY: I'm sorry, Meg, I didn't realise— [you'd feel this way.]
MEG: [*interrupting*] And I thought we told each other everything.
LUCY: [*itching to blurt it out*] It's not that I lied to you. I just didn't tell you.
MEG: *You're* the one who always says that deliberately not telling something is the same as lying.

> *This is torture for* LUCY. *The door opens and* COLLEEN *re-enters in her nightie. Her tone is scolding, as though she's talking to ten-year-old kids.*

COLLEEN: What's going on in here? You girls should be well and truly in bed by now.
MEG: Oh, sorry, Mum. Did we wake you up? We're playing Truth or Dare.
COLLEEN: Truth or—don't be silly, Margaret. Come on, quickly, into bed. Do you want to look exhausted tomorrow?
MEG: Hardly.

> *Pushing the other two off,* MEG *climbs under the blankets.*

Get off, you two. Alright, Mum. I'm in bed.

> LUCY *jumps onto the folding bed.*

LUCY: So am I. 'Night, Colleen… [*Pointedly*] 'Night, Angela.

> ANGELA *looks between them, worried that* LUCY *will spill the beans.*

ANGELA: I think I'll sleep out here with you two.
COLLEEN: Don't be silly. There's a free bed in the next room.
ANGELA: [*jumping in beside* MEG] Yeah, but there's plenty of room in here with Meg—

MEG: I'm a kicker, Ange. You'd have bruises under your bridesmaid's dress.
ANGELA: I don't mind.

But COLLEEN'*s already pulling back the bedclothes. She practically drags* ANGELA *out of the bed.*

COLLEEN: [*scolding*] Don't be silly, Angela. You'll see the girls in the morning.
LUCY: [*pointedly*] Yeah. We'll see you in the morning.
ANGELA: [*thwarted*] Alright then…
MEG: 'Night, Ange. Sleep well.
ANGELA: 'Night, Meg. 'Night, Lucy— [*Throwing a final warning look at* LUCY, *a joke laced with sub-text*] Don't do anything I wouldn't do.

And with that she turns, and mustering all the drunken dignity she can, opens the door and exits—straight into the wardrobe. She emerges, embarrassed, and scuttles off to the second bedroom.

Meanwhile COLLEEN *has turned off the main light and is heading for* MEG'*s bed.*

COLLEEN: 'Night, then…
MEG: Night, Mum.

COLLEEN *gives* MEG *a kiss, and then in a spontaneous rush of maternal tenderness, she starts tucking in the bedclothes.* MEG *is amused and surprised.*

Mum?
COLLEEN: Let's tuck you in, nice and tight.

She tucks her in.

There you are, snug as a bug in a rug. Now sleep tight till morning bright. Your very last night as a single girl…
MEG: [*touched*] Yeah…

As COLLEEN *walks past* LUCY, *there's an awkward moment where she's not sure whether she should tuck her in or not. She pauses, does a little two-step.*

LUCY: I'm all tucked. Thanks, Colleen.
COLLEEN: [*relieved*] Alright, well, goodnight then.
LUCY: 'Night.

MEG: 'Night, Mum. Sleep well…

>COLLEEN *exits.*

>MEG *pops her head up above the bedclothes and grins across at* LUCY.

Can you turn the light off, Luce? I'm trapped here.

>*Her head pops down again.*

LUCY: [*grinning*] Sure…

>*She sits up to turn off the lamp between the beds, but she doesn't flick the switch.*

Listen, I'm sorry I didn't tell you about that girl…

MEG: It's okay… I was just surprised… I didn't think we kept anything from each other…

LUCY: I didn't *deliberately* keep it from you.

MEG: [*mildly*] Oh, come on, Luce… You did it with a woman. It's not like you would've forgotten.

LUCY: Yeah, alright. I suppose I was embarrassed.

MEG: Why? With *me*? *I* wouldn't care.

LUCY: Yeah. I know, but I guess I just—

MEG: [*overlapping*] Look, anyway, I don't want to make a big deal of it, but I was surprised 'cause I've always loved how you don't censor yourself—

LUCY: [*interjecting*] Yeah, but—

MEG: [*over her*] You know me, I'm always watching what I say—not with you, but with everyone else—'cause I don't want to hurt their feelings or I'm worried about what they'll think, but you just come straight out with it. You're not scared to say things that people don't want to hear. That's one of the things I love about you.

LUCY: [*this is torture*] Thanks.

MEG: Anyway, you're officially forgiven. Can you turn off the light? If I don't get eight hours I'll have bags under my eyes.

LUCY: Sure.

>LUCY *turns off the light and lies down. The stage is in darkness, save for the city view through the window. Voices from the darkness:*

MEG: Goodnight, you big lezzo.

LUCY: 'Night.

A long silence in the darkness, then…
 Meg…
MEG: Mmm…?
LUCY: James has been having an affair.

END OF ACT ONE

ACT TWO

SCENE EIGHT

It's the next morning. About 7.15 a.m.

The hotel room is empty except for a hung-over ANGELA, *who is freshly showered and wears her bridesmaid's dress. She drops a Berocca into a glass of water as she talks on the phone.*

ANGELA: [*into the phone*] Yeah, he's been sleeping with Naomi Bartlett! She's invited to the wedding, and everything! No, she threw Lucy out at about midnight. No, her mum doesn't know anything, and Meg doesn't know I know… [*Looking around, she winces as the movement hurts her head.*] I'm not sure. They weren't here when I got up… but I thought I should get dressed in case… But I just wanted to ring and… tell you how much I love you and…

A key is heard in the door, and COLLEEN*'s voice.*

COLLEEN: [*off*] Oh, I've just thought—!
ANGELA: [*into the phone, hastily*] Got to go! 'Bye!

> ANGELA *slams the phone down as the door opens and* MEG *and* COLLEEN *enter. They're both extremely agitated, especially* MEG. COLLEEN *is wearing her Mother-of-the-Bride outfit.*

COLLEEN: [*to* MEG, *as they enter*] The seating at Table Eleven—!
MEG: [*over her, to* ANGELA, *curtly*] Has James rung?
ANGELA: No.
MEG: Shit.

She stomps straight over to the phone.

COLLEEN: Oh, Angela, you're dressed. You look lovely.
ANGELA: Thanks, Mrs Bacon. So do you.

> *Meanwhile* MEG *punches some numbers aggressively into the phone.* COLLEEN *maintains her forced cheer. She's nervy, on edge.*

COLLEEN: We've just been downstairs giving Meg's father the name cards. Jenny's going to get some extra ribbon—
ANGELA: Great. So it's all under control— [*then?*]

COLLEEN: [*overlapping, to* MEG] Anyway, as I was saying—this means we *can* invite your Great Uncle Reg— But how are we going to explain inviting him at the last minute?
MEG: [*agitated, into the phone*] Be there… be there… be there…
COLLEEN: And we can't put him at Table Eleven—
MEG: [*overlapping*] Ssshh! Shit! [*Listening impatiently to James' outgoing message*] James, it's me again for the fiftieth time. Why haven't you turned this thing back on yet? Can you call me at the hotel or on my mobile? 'Bye. [*She hangs up.*] Shit. Shit. Shit. [*To* COLLEEN, *re: the language*] Sorry.
COLLEEN: [*wincing*] It's alright.
ANGELA: Meg, are you okay?
MEG: [*overlapping, tersely*] No! But I don't want to talk about it.
COLLEEN: Neither do we, Sweetheart. Not if *you* don't. Now, I'm thinking we could move the Radners from Table Four to Table Eleven and put Great Uncle Reg and the vegetarian at Table Four—
MEG: [*irritably*] Whatever—
ANGELA: Can I get anyone a cup of tea—?
COLLEEN: Do you think your cousin Mark would have left Ballarat yet?
MEG: How would I know?
COLLEEN: He could pick up Uncle Reg on the way— But why should some vegetarian we've never met be at Table Four—?

But meanwhile MEG *has caught sight of herself in a silver lid from the room service breakfast. She lifts it up, stares into it in horror.*

MEG: Mum, I don't care! Shit, look at me. I look terrible.
ANGELA: No you don't.
COLLEEN: You look beautiful, Meg—
MEG: Oh, come on! I've got bags under my eyes and I'm white as a… a ghost—
COLLEEN: [*more and more uptight*] You look lovely—!
MEG: [*overlapping, almost yelling*] I look disgusting—!
COLLEEN: All you need's a bit of make-up—
MEG: And how am I supposed to keep that on?! I can't stop crying! [*Blowing her nose loudly*] I'm going to look haggard walking up the aisle. And everyone will think, 'She should be glowing, but she's a wreck. What's happened?'
COLLEEN: Just a *little bit* of make-up—!

MEG: I don't need make-up! I need a fucking miracle!

> COLLEEN *cringes at the language as the phone rings.* MEG *leaps for it instantly.*

Thank God!

> *Their uptight energy is communicating itself to* ANGELA, *in spite of her best efforts. And the hang-over headache isn't helping.*

ANGELA: [*contained tension*] Mrs Bacon? A cup of tea?
COLLEEN: [*distractedly*] Yes, alright.
MEG: [*into the phone*] James?! Oh, hi Dad. Yeah, we're getting ready—
ANGELA: Earl Grey or English Breakfast?
MEG: [*snarling into the phone*] Nothing! I'm fine! Yeah, hang on a second— [*Holding the phone out to* COLLEEN, *angrily*] What did you say to him?!
COLLEEN: [*lying*] I didn't say anything!
MEG: It's something about the ribbons. And keep it short.

> COLLEEN *takes the phone from* MEG. MEG *stomps away and gets a packet of bandaids from her toiletries bag.*

ANGELA: Mrs Bacon? English Breakfast?
COLLEEN: [*ignoring her, into the phone*] Yes Bill…? [*Lowering her voice*] Yes, she's still upset… No, I don't know— [*why.*]
MEG: [*overlapping: Shut up!*] Mum!

> ANGELA *has interpreted the 'yes' and 'no' as conflicting responses to her tea bag question. As* COLLEEN's *conversation continues, she waves two tea bags in front of her face, hoping for a response that doesn't come.*

COLLEEN: [*into the phone*] Anyway—the ribbons? No, I said I want Jenny to tie them… What? But Spotlight doesn't open for another forty-five minutes—there's no point waiting out the front now—can you go and get her?
ANGELA: [*sighing*] I'll make you an English breakfast, then.
COLLEEN: [*into the phone*] Now listen, I need you to ring Uncle Reg and invite him. But first ring Mark and ask if he can pick Uncle Reg up on his way through from Ballarat. And you'll need to go to the reception centre and move the place cards—put the Radners on Table Eleven and Uncle Reg and—ah— [*Turning to* MEG] What's the vegetarian's name?
MEG: [*snarling*] How should I know?!

COLLEEN: [*snarling back*] I'm only asking, Margaret! [*Back on the phone*] Hold on, Bill—

> *She hurries over, grumpily grabs the seating plan and goes back to the phone.* ANGELA *is really tense now too. She's boiling the kettle.*

ANGELA: You want a cup of tea, Meg?

MEG: [*overlapping, looking in the mirror*] Look at that. I've got broken capillaries all over my face—

ANGELA: No you haven't. You haven't got any.

MEG: Bullshit, Ange. I'm covered in them.

COLLEEN: [*into the phone*] His name's Paul Whelan—I don't know *who* the man is, Bill, let's not get into that—

MEG: [*waving the bandaids aggressively*] And to top it all off, I can't even *walk* in my bloody wedding shoes!

> *She's unwrapping large bandaids to put on her ankle.*

COLLEEN: [*into the phone*] Anyway, put him on Table Four with Uncle Reg— No, I can't leave him on Table Eleven because that would mean separating the Graingers!

> ANGELA *takes a cup of tea over to* COLLEEN *and waits for her to finish her call.*

[*Into the phone*] Yes, alright. Good. Right. We'll see you soon then. 'Bye.

> *She hangs up just in time to see* MEG *unwrapping the bandaids. She pushes past* ANGELA*, ignoring the cup of tea she's made for her.* ANGELA*'s getting grumpy now.*

[*Snapping, shocked*] What are you doing?!

MEG: What does it look like I'm doing?! I'm putting a bandaid on my ankle!

COLLEEN: You can't put a bandaid on your ankle! People will see it when you do the bridal waltz!

MEG: But I won't be able to do the bridal waltz if I don't! My bloody shoes kill me!

COLLEEN: I told you to wear them around the house!

MEG: I did. That's when I got the blisters!

COLLEEN: Well, for heaven's sake, Margaret! Why didn't you buy transparent bandaids?!

MEG: There's no such thing!

COLLEEN: There is so! Angela, can't you buy transparent bandaids?!

ANGELA can't contain herself any longer. She's thoroughly drawn into the argument.

ANGELA: Those ones are fine. They're flesh-coloured.

COLLEEN: They're not flesh-coloured! *Look* at them! They don't match her ankle!

ANGELA: [*grumpily*] I think they do!

COLLEEN: Oh, rubbish! They're a totally different shade of beige!

MEG: [*screaming*] Well, I'm sorry if my ankle's the wrong colour, Mum! Why don't I just *paint* my ankle?!

ANGELA: [*muttering to herself*] Bloody Lucy! I *knew* this would happen!

COLLEEN: [*over* ANGELA, *trying to calm* MEG] Oh look, it'll be alright. We'll just have to make do with—

But MEG *isn't listening. She can't believe what she's just heard.*

MEG: [*interrupting, to* ANGELA] What did you say?!

ANGELA'*s expression says it all: Ooops, busted.*

What did you say just then?

ANGELA: Nothing. I was just saying it's a shame that you and Lucy—

MEG: [*overlapping*] You *knew* about it, didn't you—?! [*Turning on* COLLEEN] Did you know too?!

COLLEEN: Know what?

MEG/ANGELA: [*snapping in unison*] Nothing!

An awkward silence as COLLEEN *looks from* MEG *to* ANGELA, *not sure what to do with herself.*

COLLEEN: I'm sure the bouquets should be here by now. I might just ring Reception and check. I'll just—I think I'll do that from *my* room.

And she hastily exits, leaving MEG *staring at* ANGELA *in shock.*

MEG: I can't believe this…

ANGELA: I'm so sorry, Meg. I told Lucy not to tell you—

MEG: You *what?!*

ANGELA: If it was up to me, we wouldn't have told you. I know how you feel about it—

MEG: [*overlapping*] You wouldn't have *told me?!* How could you know something like this and not tell me?!

This stops ANGELA *in her tracks. She's totally flummoxed.*

ANGELA: But I thought you wouldn't want to— [know.]
MEG: [*overlapping*] I can't believe you were going to keep me in the dark. I thought you were my friend.
ANGELA: [*flummoxed*] But I *am*—
MEG: Huh. Some friend.
ANGELA: But… but… you threw Lucy out for telling you.
MEG: At least she showed me some respect. You were going to let me look like a fool on my wedding day.
ANGELA: I'm sorry, Meg… I didn't see it that way…
MEG: Well, that's how *I* see it.
ANGELA: But… You told me not to tell John…
MEG: So? That was John. This is James. This is *me,* Ange.
ANGELA: So you do want to know?
MEG: Yes. No. I don't know. Oh, what the hell would I know? I just… I don't like people knowing stuff about my life that *I* don't…
ANGELA: Of course not… I'm sorry, Meg. I thought I was doing the right thing…
MEG: Oh, I know you did, but… if there's ever anything else I should know, I want you to tell me, okay?
ANGELA: [*nodding*] Of course.
MEG: You'll tell me?

>ANGELA *reaches across and takes her hand.*

ANGELA: Of course I will.

>*They smile at each other sadly as* COLLEEN *re-enters somewhat tentatively.*

COLLEEN: Well, the bouquets aren't here yet, but I'm sure they're not far away… Why don't I help you with that bandaid, Sweetheart?
MEG: Thanks, Mum.

>COLLEEN *walks over to* MEG *with forced cheer, determined to keep things nice.*

COLLEEN: You know, now that I look at it, you can't even notice it.

>*There's a knock at the door.* ANGELA *looks at the door, still a bit dazed.*

ANGELA: I'll get that.

>*She starts walking towards the door.*

COLLEEN: It'll be the bouquets.
MEG: [*overlapping*] Or it could be Naomi Bartlett.

    ANGELA *stops dead in her tracks. Did she really hear that?*

ANGELA: *What?*
MEG: Naomi's going to step in for Lucy.
ANGELA: What…?
COLLEEN: Oh, didn't we tell you? Naomi's taking Lucy's place.
ANGELA: *Naomi* is…?
MEG: Yeah.
ANGELA: Naomi *who, again…?*
MEG: Naomi Bartlett.
ANGELA: [*weakly*] Naomi Bartlett's going to be a bridesmaid…?
MEG: [*getting impatient*] Yes.
ANGELA: But… she's not a *close* friend of yours.
MEG: I know, but Sarah's pregnant and Jenny's too small for the dress—Rachel's way too tall and Emma's breast-feeding. Naomi's exactly the right size—I'm just lucky that she said yes.

    There is another knock at the door. ANGELA *still doesn't move.*

COLLEEN: For heaven's sake, Angela, will you let her in?
ANGELA: Yeah… ah, right… of course…

    ANGELA *walks to the door, unable to believe the awfulness of the situation. She's officially in hell as she opens the door to an attractive woman in her late twenties,* NAOMI.

    NAOMI*'s forced smile is only just managing to hide her extreme nervousness.*

NAOMI: Hi!
ANGELA: [*icily*] Hi.

    ANGELA*'s hostile greeting sends* NAOMI *into a panic that she has to try and hide.*

MEG: Naomi, hi! You've met Ange before, haven't you?
NAOMI: [*nervously smiling*] Yeah, hi Angela…
MEG: And this is my mum Colleen…

    COLLEEN *walks over and shakes* NAOMI*'s hand.*

COLLEEN: [*warmly*] Nice to meet you, Naomi.
NAOMI: Nice to meet you too, Mrs Bacon.

COLLEEN: Oh, call me Colleen.

MEG: [*re: herself and* COLLEEN] Will you excuse us for just one sec? We've got a bandaid situation—

NAOMI: Yeah, sure…

>COLLEEN *goes back to* MEG *and starts applying the bandaid. Meanwhile* NAOMI *does everything she can to avoid meeting* ANGELA*'s eyes. But* ANGELA *comes around to stand in front of her, giving her a completely unambiguous look: I know what's going on.*

>*While* MEG *and* COLLEEN *are occupied with the bandaid, the following conversation takes place between* ANGELA *and* NAOMI*, via gestures and lip-reading: 'What the hell are you doing here?!' 'I couldn't get out of it! I couldn't say no!' 'Get out!' 'I'd love to, but how can I?!'*

>MEG *and* COLLEEN *are oblivious to all this because they're talking bandaids.*

MEG: Mum, that's crooked!

COLLEEN: Well, hold your foot still!

MEG: It *is* still!

COLLEEN: And it's *not* crooked, Meg—

MEG: It's on a forty-five-degree angle! Look!

COLLEEN: Alright, alright—

>*She pulls the bandaid off.*

MEG: Oww!

COLLEEN: Don't be silly, Margaret. That didn't hurt.

>*She re-applies the bandaid at a straight angle.*

There you are. Alright?

MEG: Yes. Thank you.

COLLEEN: All done.

>*They both turn their attention to* NAOMI. ANGELA *feels she has to do something.*

ANGELA: Meg—

>*But* MEG *walks straight past her to* NAOMI*, warm and welcoming.*

MEG: [*overlapping*] Thanks for getting here so quickly, Naomi—

NAOMI: Glad I could help.

MEG: [*kissing her*] You're a lifesaver—!
ANGELA: [*interrupting, tightly*] Meg, can I talk to you for a second? Alone?
MEG: [*distracted*] What…?
ANGELA: Can I talk to you for a second? In private?
MEG: What about—?
NAOMI: [*interrupting, desperately cheerful*] So, how are preparations going?!
COLLEEN: Not as quickly as they should be—
ANGELA: [*to* MEG] I just want to talk to you for one second—
COLLEEN: [*interrupting, briskly*] There's been far too much gossiping already, girls. Look at the time—!
MEG: [*looking at her watch*] Oh yeah, you're right, Mum—
ANGELA: It'll only take a couple of seconds—
MEG: Not now, Ange.
ANGELA: [*overlapping*] But I really need to—
COLLEEN: Not *now,* Angela! We need to get Naomi dressed—
MEG: [*playfully*] And somebody else.
COLLEEN: Oh, Sweetheart, as if we'd forget the bride…!
ANGELA: [*interrupting, desperately*] But—it's not going to fit!

    MEG *and* COLLEEN *stop and look at* ANGELA *in surprise.*

MEG: What?
ANGELA: The dress! She's taller than Lucy. Aren't you, Naomi?

    NAOMI*'s just as keen to get out of there as* ANGELA *is to have her leave.*

NAOMI: Yeah, I am a lot taller—!
MEG: You're not *a lot* taller—
ANGELA: The dress is going to be way too short.
NAOMI: Yeah, I wouldn't want to spoil the effect—
MEG: A couple of inches won't make any difference.
ANGELA: But her ankles will show. It'll look untidy.

    COLLEEN *visibly reacts to this horrific scenario.* NAOMI *seizes on it.*

NAOMI: I'd hate to make the wedding party look untidy. Maybe you should just have one bridesmaid—?
ANGELA: Yeah, I think it'd be better to just have one—!
COLLEEN: [*nearing the end of her tether*] We *can't* have *one* bridesmaid because that would mean only having *one* groomsman, and we can't

get hold of James to tell him. And there's only a slight difference in height anyway, so... [*smiling maternally at all three*] I suggest that we all relax and enjoy Meg's special day together, because that's all that counts, isn't it...?

>MEG *smiles back. In spite of everything, she really wants to enjoy this morning.*

MEG: Yeah, you're right, Mum. I've been waiting thirty-three years for this, so let's just have some fun, eh?

>NAOMI *and* ANGELA *give strangled smiles in return.*

ANGELA/NAOMI: Yeah. / Yeah, of course. / Great. [*etc.*]

COLLEEN: Just slip off your shoes for us, will you, Naomi...?

>*Meanwhile* ANGELA *gives it one more try.*

ANGELA: [*low*] Meg...

>*But* MEG *silences her with a warm hug.*

MEG: It's alright... Just don't do it to me again.

>ANGELA *smiles limply as* MEG *breaks the hug and starts heading to the wardrobe.*

Now let's get you into this dress, Naomi.

COLLEEN: [*following her*] But maybe we should try the shoes first.

MEG: Mum, can you relax about the shoes? Please? I think the dress is a bit more important.

>*As* COLLEEN *and* MEG *fuss over at the wardrobe,* ANGELA *gestures frantically for* NAOMI *to leave while they're not looking.* NAOMI *runs to the door, then remembers her handbag, running back to pick it up just as* MEG *looks over.*

Okay, Naomi, get your gear off.

>*Thwarted,* NAOMI *starts taking off her skirt and top. Meanwhile* MEG *and* COLLEEN *are fussing with the bridesmaid's dress.*

COLLEEN: Slip it off the hanger carefully, Meg. We don't want to crumple it— [*Looking at the dress, then over at* NAOMI] Oh, I'm sure it'll fit...

>NAOMI *slips off her skirt and top to reveal beautiful French lingerie (the kind a woman buys when she's met a new man).*

MEG: Wooh... gorgeous undies. Who's the lucky guy?

NAOMI: [*smiling awkwardly*] What?! Oh, no-one.

> *She tries to grab the bridesmaid's dress, but* MEG *playfully holds it out of reach as she teases her for more information.*

MEG: [*playfully*] Come off it. You don't buy this kind of stuff for *yourself.* You would have had to mortgage your flat for this. Who is he, and how come I haven't heard about him?

NAOMI: [*grabbing the dress*] Oh, it was just a guy. And it's over, anyway.

ANGELA: [*dripping with sarcasm*] Oh, what a shame.

> NAOMI *slips the dress over her head, managing to disappear for a precious second. Meanwhile* MEG *and* COLLEEN *look a little surprised by* ANGELA'*s tone, but there are too many other things to worry about.*

COLLEEN: Well, quickly, help her. Come on, Meg—

> MEG *and* COLLEEN *help* NAOMI *slip the dress down over her.*

NAOMI: It feels like it should fit...

ANGELA: [*pointedly*] Does it really?

NAOMI: [*oops*] Well, no, ah, no, maybe not.

COLLEEN: Don't be silly. It's going to be fine!

MEG: Let's do up the zip before we say that, Mum... Ange...?

ANGELA: What? Oh, sure... I'll just...

> ANGELA *starts doing up the zip, 'accidentally' pinching* NAOMI'*s skin in the process.*

NAOMI: Ouch!

ANGELA: [*totally insincere*] Sorry.

> ANGELA *fastens the zip right up to the top. The dress looks to be quite a good fit.*

MEG: Oh, it's pretty good, thank God!

COLLEEN: What did I tell you? It looks fine.

ANGELA: I still think it's way too short.

NAOMI: Yeah, I think it might be too short too.

> COLLEEN *and* MEG *stand back and look at the dress length appraisingly.*

MEG: No. It's lovely, isn't it, Mum?

COLLEEN: It's fine. Turn around for us, Naomi—

NAOMI *does a quick turn around in a circle.* MEG *and* COLLEEN *like what they see.*

No, that length is fine...

MEG: It's lovely.

COLLEEN: And thank goodness for that! Now let's see if the shoes fit. Angela, can you get Lucy's shoes please?

ANGELA: [*sullenly*] Yes.

As ANGELA *stomps over to the wardrobe and grabs Lucy's shoes...*

MEG: [*to* NAOMI] Show us your feet— Oh, they look about right...

COLLEEN: Yes, the shoes should be fine...

ANGELA *makes a point of staring at* NAOMI*'s feet.*

ANGELA: You reckon? Her feet are much fatter than Lucy's.

She thrusts the shoes at NAOMI *with such force that she almost falls over backwards.*

[*As she thrusts the shoes*] Here.

NAOMI: [*almost falling over*] Oh—!

COLLEEN: Careful, Angela.

ANGELA: Sorry, Naomi.

MEG *and* COLLEEN *look at* ANGELA *in bemusement, but don't comment. Meanwhile* COLLEEN *is taking Lucy's shoes out of the box.*

COLLEEN: Well, quickly, let's try them on—

She hands the shoes to NAOMI. *In spite of the awfulness of the situation, in true female fashion* NAOMI *finds herself captivated by the shoes.*

NAOMI: Oh, wow... they're beautiful....

MEG: You like them?

NAOMI: Yeah, they're gorgeous... And I love the shine...

COLLEEN*'s lips instantly purse and* MEG *rolls her eyes in amusement.*

[*Puzzled*] What...?

MEG: Don't get Mum started on the shiny part. It's a tad controversial.

NAOMI: Oh... Well, here goes...

MEG: Good luck, Cinderella...

COLLEEN: Quickly. Do they fit—?

They all watch anxiously as NAOMI *slips her foot into the shoe. She wiggles it around.*

NAOMI: Yeah, they fit—
MEG: Phew.
COLLEEN: Thank Goodness for that—!
ANGELA: [*through gritted teeth*] They don't look like they fit.
NAOMI: [*oops again*] Well, actually, maybe, yeah now that I—yeah, I think they're a fraction too big.
COLLEEN: Where are they too big? In the toes?
NAOMI: [*walking a few steps*] Yeah, mainly in the toes.

COLLEEN *starts briskly heading for the bathroom.* ANGELA *follows, calling after her.*

ANGELA: Well, we can't have a bridesmaid with shoes that don't fit—
COLLEEN: [*overlapping*] Rubbish. We'll just use a bit of tissue—

She emerges from the bathroom with a roll of toilet paper.

MEG: [*joking*] Mum's the improviser from hell.

COLLEEN *plonks herself on the end of the bed and starts ripping up the toilet paper.* MEG *sits down beside her.*

COLLEEN: Here, give me the shoes, Naomi—

NAOMI *gives her the shoes.* COLLEEN *passes one to* MEG, *then demonstrates.* MEG *follows her lead.*

Now, if we just… pull off the paper, then fold it like this… and put a little in the toe of the shoes… like so…

During this, NAOMI *and* ANGELA *are exchanging silent looks.* NAOMI'*s look says: 'I hate this as much as you do, but I can't get out of it now'.*

And that should fill up the gap— [*Handing the shoes back*] Here, Naomi, try that.

NAOMI *puts the shoes back on with difficulty, and walks a few stilted, slow steps. They're way too tight now, and they're causing her pain.*

NAOMI: [*trying to turn a painful grimace to a smile*] That's great, Mrs Bacon. Yeah… They feel fine now…
COLLEEN: Oh, good.
MEG: You're a genius, Mum.

COLLEEN: Well, what a relief... The dress *and* the shoes!

MEG suddenly gets a little emotional as she looks at NAOMI *and* ANGELA *in their matching bridesmaids' outfits. She nudges her mother.*

MEG: Oh, look...

They both gaze at NAOMI *and* ANGELA, *moved.*

I just want to say... when Lucy got food poisoning I didn't know what I was going to do... I'm so glad you said yes at such short notice... I know this is a big ask, Naomi, and I really appreciate it.

MEG emotionally pulls NAOMI *into a hug. Then she pulls* ANGELA *into the hug too.*

ANGELA *can't resist another deeply sarcastic comment.*

ANGELA: Yeah. You're such a *good friend*, Naomi.

COLLEEN *notes* ANGELA's *sarcasm. She claps briskly to break up the hug.*

COLLEEN: Come on, girls! The clock's ticking!

As the hug breaks, COLLEEN *excitedly turns to* MEG.

It's time for you to get dressed, Sweetheart!

MEG: Okay. I'll go grab the frumpy old frock...!

COLLEEN: [*laughing*] Oh, Meg...!

She starts walking into the next room. NAOMI *stumbles after her painfully, desperate to get away from* ANGELA's *icy gaze.*

NAOMI: Here—I'll help you!

MEG: Thanks, Naomi.

As soon as MEG *and* NAOMI *leave the room,* COLLEEN's *smile vanishes. She brusquely pulls* ANGELA *aside.*

COLLEEN: [*hissing, low*] What in heaven's name are you doing?

ANGELA: What do you mean?

COLLEEN: Why are you being so horrible?

ANGELA: I'm not.

COLLEEN: Yes you are. You're being nasty to poor Naomi.

ANGELA: 'Poor' Naomi?

COLLEEN: Yes. Poor Naomi. She's doing Meg a big favour in case you hadn't noticed.

ANGELA: [*sarcastically*] Well, isn't Meg lucky to have a friend like *her*?

> COLLEEN *is totally flummoxed by* ANGELA*'s out of character nastiness.*

COLLEEN: What's wrong? *Why* are you being so horrible?

> ANGELA *pauses for a beat, then makes a spontaneous decision.*

ANGELA: Alright, Colleen…

> COLLEEN *reacts to her Christian name.*

I'll tell you why—

> *But* COLLEEN *instantly puts her hands over her ears.*

COLLEEN: [*hastily interrupting*] I don't want to know why, I just want you to stop it. It won't kill you to be pleasant for Meg's sake.

> MEG *and* NAOMI *return with the wedding dress in its plastic cover and* MEG*'s veil.* NAOMI *looks like she's not far from tears.*

MEG: [*excitedly*] Okay, here goes. Will you help me get into this thing?

COLLEEN: Of course, Sweetheart. Come on, Angela!

> ANGELA *and* COLLEEN *unzip the wedding dress and remove it from its plastic as* MEG *starts getting undressed. Meanwhile* NAOMI *hovers, holding the veil.*

Now, be careful of the zip. We don't want to snag it—

ANGELA: Oh, it's beautiful fabric…!

COLLEEN: Yes, it's Italian silk.

> ANGELA *takes the plastic cover away and turns to see* MEG *in full bridal lingerie.*

ANGELA: [*trying to be pleasant for* MEG*'s sake*] Woooh, gorgeous…

NAOMI: [*a nervous wreck*] Yeah, gorgeous…

MEG: [*to* NAOMI] Do you think James will approve?

NAOMI: I wouldn't know! [*Collecting herself*] I mean, yeah, of course, what man wouldn't?

> NAOMI *tries to smile casually, but her lip starts trembling. During the following, she starts crying in spite of all her best efforts.* ANGELA *quickly shoves her out of the way so* MEG *won't see her tears.* COLLEEN *is oblivious. She's totally focused on the wedding dress.*

COLLEEN: Alright… if we just gently open it up like this… and put it down towards the ground… Angela, just pull that out for me, will you?
ANGELA: This bit?
COLLEEN: No, this bit. That's right. Alright, Meg, you step over the top…

In spite of the circumstances, MEG *is clearly feeling the magic of the moment.*

MEG: Here goes…
COLLEEN: Gently now… That's right, slowly… Now pull it up very gently…

ANGELA *and* COLLEEN *pull the beautiful, heavy, voluminous dress up higher.*

MEG: It's happening… I'm starting to feel like a bride…
COLLEEN: Put your arms through here, Meg, like that. No, both arms—

ANGELA *gently touches the beading on the bodice.*

ANGELA: This beading's just beautiful.
MEG: [*I know*] Isn't it gorgeous?
COLLEEN: It's exquisite…
MEG: [*with an excited laugh*] I'm *wearing* it, I can't believe it. The fittings were one thing, but this is *for real.*
COLLEEN: You're the most beautiful bride I've ever seen…
MEG: [*fondly*] You're probably a tad biased, Mum.
ANGELA: No, it's true, Meg. You look amazing.
MEG: I feel like Cinderella on her way to the ball… I know that sounds so cheesy…
ANGELA: Who cares?

MEG *and* ANGELA *share an emotional laugh.* NAOMI *sniffles loudly.* ANGELA *shoves her out of the way again, unnoticed by* COLLEEN *and* MEG. *Meanwhile* COLLEEN *tries to collect herself by getting bossy again.*

COLLEEN: Well, come on, Angela! Help me do her up.

ANGELA *and* COLLEEN *start doing up the tiny pearl buttons on the back of Meg's dress, while* NAOMI *tries to keep a low profile, quietly crying her heart out.*

ANGELA: Oh, I love these little pearl buttons…

MEG: James wanted these. He's going to undo them with his teeth one at a time… Sorry, Mum. Too many details?
COLLEEN: [*focused on the buttons*] Keep still.
MEG: Naomi, where are you hiding? What do you think?

She tries to pull away, but ANGELA *pulls her back.*

ANGELA: She loves it.

Meanwhile NAOMI *is looking for somewhere, anywhere to hide. But too late…*

MEG: I asked Naomi, Ange. [*Breaking free of* ANGELA*'s grasp*] What do you think?

Trapped, NAOMI *tries to smile, but there's no mistaking the fact that she's crying.*

NAOMI: You look beautiful, Meg…
MEG: Oh, you're crying… That's so sweet… [*Joking, to* COLLEEN *and* ANGELA] Why aren't you two ice queens crying?

At that moment there's a knock at the door.

COLLEEN: [*crying*] That'll be the bouquets—!
NAOMI: [*desperately trying to extract herself*] I'll get it!

She limps painfully to the door, desperate for a two-second breather. Meanwhile ANGELA *and* COLLEEN *resume buttoning up Meg's dress.*

COLLEEN: Thank goodness. I was starting to worry. The florist told me they'd be here by eight—

NAOMI *answers the door to an attractive man in his mid-thirties,* JAMES.

His eyes nearly pop out of his head when he sees NAOMI *in the bridesmaid's dress.*

NAOMI: James!
JAMES: [*overlapping*] Naomi?!
MEG: James!
JAMES: [*recovering himself*] Naomi. Hi.
COLLEEN: James!
MEG: James! Thank God you're here!

She rushes over to her fiancé, desperately in need of reassurance.

>COLLEEN *follows, placing herself between them and trying to block* JAMES' *view.*

COLLEEN: [*overlapping*] No, no, you shouldn't have come—!
JAMES: [*overlapping*] I got all your messages. What's wrong?
COLLEEN: [*overlapping*] It's bad luck for you to see Meg before the wedding!
MEG: M-u-u-u-m-!
COLLEEN: [*trying to push him out the door*] You can talk to her at the church—
MEG: No, Mum. I need to talk to him *now*. Privately. *Then* I'll kick him out.
COLLEEN: Alright, alright, but be quick. The photographer will be here soon. [*Then to* JAMES] And try not to look at her.
JAMES: I'll avert my eyes.
ANGELA: [*feeling sick for* MEG] Well, we'll wait next door, then.
COLLEEN: Don't be too long.

>COLLEEN *exits, followed by* ANGELA. *Meanwhile* NAOMI *stands near* JAMES *and* MEG, *frozen with terror. A couple of beats, then* ANGELA *re-emerges, and...*

ANGELA: Naomi!
NAOMI: [*jumping*] Ohh!

>NAOMI *moves quickly past* JAMES *and* MEG *and limps from the room as fast as her incredibly painful shoes will take her.*

>MEG *and* JAMES *are alone. He looks at her warily. He's got a bad feeling. But he covers.*

JAMES: I'm not having much luck averting my eyes. You look beautiful.

>*In spite of everything,* MEG *can't help glowing a little at that.*

MEG: Do you think so?
JAMES: [*nodding, absolutely genuine*] You look amazing…

>MEG*'s pleased, but when he moves to touch her, she moves away.*

MEG: I didn't know you knew Naomi.
JAMES: Yeah, I met her at netball once, remember? So what's she doing here? And where's Lucy?
NAOMI: I threw her out because she said you've been having an affair.
JAMES: What?!
MEG: She said you've been having an affair.

JAMES: What?! Where the hell did she get that from?
MEG: [*wanting desperately to believe this*] So it's not true?

> JAMES *hedges, desperate to avoid a blatant lie.*

JAMES: Meg, I love you. More than anything.
MEG: And you wouldn't betray me?
JAMES: I want to marry you, in case you hadn't noticed.

> *But* MEG *pushes, determined to get a direct answer.*

MEG: And you *promise* you've *never* had an affair?

> *The tiniest hint of a pause, then...*

JAMES: No! No, of course I haven't. How could you think I'd—? No, Meg, absolutely not.
MEG: [*after a beat*] I *want* to believe you…
JAMES: But you don't?
MEG: Well, Lucy's never lied to me before.
JAMES: I guess Lucy must think it's true—God knows why—but she's wrong.

> MEG *stares up at him, studying his face for emotional details.*

She is. I swear.

> *It's a struggle for* MEG *to believe him, and it shows. Another small silence, then...*

Meg, if you're going to believe some baseless rumour over my word, are you sure you *should* be marrying me?
MEG: Don't say that! I *want* to marry you!
JAMES: And I want to marry you too, but I need to know you trust me.
MEG: I do!
JAMES: Do you really?
MEG: Yes! Really! I do!
JAMES: You do?
MEG: I do.

> JAMES *smiles at her gently, warmly.*

JAMES: [*tenderly, teasing*] I like hearing you say that.

> MEG *melts. He pursues the advantage and put his arms around her.*

Will you say it again in a couple of hours?
MEG: I might…

JAMES: Good… Is it bad luck to kiss the bride?
MEG: Who cares?

They fall into each other's arms and exchange a long kiss, then pull apart.

JAMES: I love you, Meg.
MEG: I love you too.

Another deep smile between them, and then JAMES *starts heading for the door.*

JAMES: We'll let them in, eh?

MEG *nods. As* JAMES *turns and walks to the door, one look at his face shows how much he loathes himself right now. Meanwhile* MEG*'s ecstatic as she heads to the mirror. She's heard what she wants to hear and she's more than happy to believe it.*

[*To the others*] You can come back now…

As JAMES *opens the door and* COLLEEN, ANGELA *and* NAOMI *re-enter,* MEG *greets them with a beaming smile.* NAOMI *looks like she could crack at any second, but* MEG *is oblivious.*

MEG: Come on in, everything's fine!
COLLEEN: It's all sorted out, then?
MEG: Yeah, Mum.
COLLEEN: Oh, lovely!
ANGELA: So everything's okay?
MEG: [*nodding*] It's perfect.

ANGELA *is bemused, to say the least. How could they sort it out that quickly?*

ANGELA: Are you sure, Meg?
MEG: [*beaming*] Yeah, I'm sure.

MEG *slips her arm through* JAMES*' arm and smiles at the stunned* NAOMI, *who is hovering behind* ANGELA.

[*To* NAOMI] We *did* have a bit of 'an issue', but we've talked it through and we've resolved it.
JAMES: Yeah. Everything's fine.

He throws a barely perceptible look at NAOMI, *which she misinterprets.*

COLLEEN: Oh, I'm so glad!
MEG: So let's get ready for a wedding, eh?
COLLEEN: Lovely! [*Grabbing* JAMES *'arm*] Now *you* have to leave, young man—

> As COLLEEN *starts leading* JAMES *to the door, a deeply emotional* NAOMI *approaches* MEG.

NAOMI: This is *really* beautiful! [*Crying*] You are *so* courageous...
MEG: [*bemused*] Ah... thanks...

> JAMES *has just realised that* NAOMI *is about to blow it. As he tries to 'casually' extricate himself from* COLLEEN *at the door:*

NAOMI: And you still want me to be your bridesmaid?
MEG: [*smiling, confused*] Of course. Why wouldn't I—?

> *But* JAMES *has made it back to* MEG*'s side.*

JAMES: [*interrupting*] You know, maybe you should just have one bridesmaid?

> ANGELA *has just realised what's going on, and jumps in too.*

ANGELA: That's what I suggested before. The dress doesn't suit her—
MEG: Angela!
JAMES: Look, I don't want to offend Naomi, but I agree. It looks sort of funny—
MEG: James—!
JAMES: What do you think, Colleen?
COLLEEN: [*worried*] I think it looks fine. You think it looks funny?
JAMES: [*darting* NAOMI *warning looks*] No offence, Naomi, I know it's rude to say this when I've only met you *once before*, but—

> NAOMI *suddenly gets the message: Meg doesn't know.*

NAOMI: Oh! Oh! Okay. Yeah. I think you're right. The colour's the problem.
COLLEEN: What's wrong with the colour?
NAOMI: It washes me out.
MEG: No it doesn't—
ANGELA: It does! She looks like a corpse.
NAOMI: I think you'd better just have one bridesmaid.
MEG: No, I'm having *two!* I don't know what's got into these people, but I apologise for their appalling manners. You look gorgeous. Doesn't she, Mum?

COLLEEN: Yes, beautiful. And besides, we don't have time to rearrange the bridal table.

> *Underneath all this,* JAMES *and* NAOMI *have been communicating wordlessly.*

JAMES: Alright, I've been told. I'm sorry if I offended you, Naomi.
MEG: I should think so. [*Gently pushing* JAMES] Now get out of here. We've got a wedding to get to.
JAMES: Consider me gone. [*Holding his hands in front of his eyes so he can't see*] See, Colleen? Not looking.
COLLEEN: [*giggling girlishly*] Ohhh, James…

> *But as* JAMES *passes* NAOMI*, he trips and loses his balance. She instinctively reaches out to steady him and they end up tangled in each other's arms, unwittingly embracing.*

JAMES: Ohh!
MEG: Careful!
NAOMI: Ohhh!
JAMES: Sorry! Sorry about that, Naomi…

> NAOMI *suddenly bursts into floods of tears as she meets* JAMES' *eyes.*

NAOMI: I can't do this!
JAMES: [*deliberately misunderstanding*] Of course you can. Forget what I said. The dress looks great—
NAOMI: No, I meant I can't do this anymore!
MEG: Do what?

> JAMES *manages to free himself and start heading for the door.*

JAMES: Nothing. I don't know. See you at the church—!
NAOMI: [*overlapping*] I've been having an affair with James! I'm so sorry!

> COLLEEN *sinks into a chair, stunned.* MEG *stands transfixed. A long silence, then…*

MEG: Oh, fuck…

> *She lunges at* JAMES*, pummelling him with her fists.*

[*Yelling, crying*] You lying bastard! You lying fucking bastard!
JAMES: Meg—Meg—listen—!
MEG: [*to* NAOMI] Get out of here!

NAOMI: I'm so sorry—
MEG: [*yelling at* JAMES] And you—you get out of here too!
> She lunges at NAOMI.

Now! [*A thought occurs*] But don't go together! [*Another thought, to* JAMES] No, you stay!
NAOMI: [*trying to approach her*] I didn't mean for this to happen—!
MEG: Get the dress off! Go on, take it off now! [*To* COLLEEN *and* ANGELA] Take it off her!
> COLLEEN *and* ANGELA *descend on the sobbing* NAOMI *and very quickly relieve her of the bridesmaid's dress. Meanwhile…*

JAMES: Meg, I can explain this—
MEG: I thought you already did! [*Yelling to* ANGELA *and* COLLEEN] And take those shiny shoes off her too!
> *She hurries to* NAOMI, *who now only wears the expensive French underwear, and starts literally pushing her out the door.* NAOMI *has time to grab her handbag, but her clothes are left behind.*

[*To* JAMES] Nice underwear, isn't it? No doubt you've already seen it! [*Shoving* NAOMI *to the door*] Get out! Go on, get out—! And don't ever come near me again!
> NAOMI *runs out the door in her underwear.* MEG *slams it after her, then collapses on the bed, sobbing.* JAMES *kneels beside the bed as* COLLEEN *hurries to the other side.*

COLLEEN: Sweetheart… Oh, Sweetheart… [*Turning on* JAMES] Get out of here!
JAMES: Colleen, please—
COLLEEN: I said get out!
JAMES: I need to talk to Meg alone—
COLLEEN: I'm not leaving her alone with you. How could you do this to her?
JAMES: Can you just give us a few minutes—?
COLLEEN: You should be down on your knees thanking God you've got a girl like Meg, but *this* is how you behave—
JAMES: Please, Colleen. I need to explain it to her.
COLLEEN: You can't explain something like this. People will be arriving in an hour. [*To* MEG] Should I call your father and tell him to cancel—?

MEG: [*overlapping, sobbing*] Mum, just give us a few minutes. It's okay. I need to talk to him. Please.

> *As* COLLEEN *hovers reluctantly,* ANGELA *takes her arm.*

ANGELA: Come on, Mrs Bacon…

> COLLEEN *shrugs* ANGELA *off, but reluctantly turns to leave. She looks daggers at* JAMES *as they pass. Perhaps* ANGELA*'s look contains the tiniest hint of empathy—but not much.*

COLLEEN: I'm ashamed of you.

ANGELA: Well, it was worth it, wasn't it? We'll be downstairs, Meg.

> ANGELA *and* COLLEEN *exit.*

JAMES: Meg… Meg?

> MEG *puts a pillow over her head, refusing to hear him.* JAMES *hesitates a moment, then turns towards the audience, filled with guilt, anger and loathing—all directed squarely at himself.*
>
> *Lights fade into:*

SCENE NINE

Spotlight on JAMES *as he addresses the audience, knowing they hate him as much as he hates himself right now, and trying in vain to explain the indefensible.*

JAMES: [*grasping at straws*] Look, sex and love are separate things… Well, they can be, that's all I'm saying. This thing with Naomi—okay, it should never have happened—but it didn't have to impact on what I have with Meg. I thought that was the deal. It was a separate arrangement. She told me she just wanted a bit of fun, and now she turns around and does this…! I mean, where the hell did that come from? If I'd known Naomi felt like that I would've broken it off with her months ago— [*A beat as he realises: Who is he kidding?*] Well, maybe. Oh shit, maybe not. But I just—I just— [*A short silence as he struggles with his confusion.*] I just wish women would say what they mean. You know—plainly, clearly state what they want instead of expecting you to be psychic. Meg bought me this t-shirt at the Warner Brothers store, and it's got a picture of Superman on it. He's wearing this perplexed expression and he's saying, 'You want me to leap tall buildings *and* be sensitive and supportive?!' That's how it is with women. They want you to slay a dragon for them one second, then cry at a guide dog commercial the next. And somehow you're expected to guess when they want you to be controlling and when they want you to be crying—and if you don't make the right guess at the right time it's instantly construed as proof that you don't love them enough. 'If you really loved me, you wouldn't need to ask.' How many times have I heard that? Well, I'm sorry, I've loved a few people a lot, but no-one's ever stepped out of the shadows and handed me a crystal ball. [*He sighs—he hates himself for making excuses.*] Anyway, I know I'm trying to change the subject. The fact is, I've been acting like a prick.

Lights fade.

SCENE TEN

The door bursts open and NAOMI *re-enters in a hotel bathrobe. In tears and clutching soggy tissues, she addresses the audience directly.*

NAOMI: I had to walk down to Reception in my undies, because I was too scared to go back in there and ask for my clothes! And you know what? Even though I felt so guilty and so ashamed, I still found myself thinking 'Thank God I didn't wear that old blue bra and the baggy Cottontails'. Does that make me a bad person? Oh, I don't know. Maybe I already was… When I was younger I never thought I'd have an affair with *anyone's* boyfriend… let alone a friend's boyfriend… let alone a friend's *fiancé*... But things seem really simple when you're young—everything's so black and white. But as soon as life gets interesting it starts to turn to grey. I didn't know he was Meg's fiancé when I met him… I was drunk and he was cute and what happened happened… and then I found out he was engaged, but I really liked him by then. I tried to end it but… well, I didn't… and I kind of convinced myself—and him—that it was cool, that I could handle it, I just wanted some fun with no strings attached… And then, well, then I got Meg's wedding invitation—and that's how I found out it was him! [*Pause as she remembers the awful moment.*] Can you *believe* it? *I* couldn't. I just, I didn't know what to do, and… [*Looking at the audience guiltily*] Oh look, I know what you're thinking. I shouldn't have accepted the invitation. And maybe I shouldn't have. But I couldn't help it. I wanted James to look around the church and see my face and feel like the bastard he was—at least, that's what I told myself. But when he ended things two weeks ago I realised I'd been secretly hoping that when it came to the crunch he'd say to the priest, 'I can't go through with this. The woman I *really* love is sitting over there!' Dumb fantasy, huh? And awful to Meg. Sometimes I look at myself in the mirror and think, 'With friends like me, who needs enemies?' But you know how sometimes when you need it most you can't get your head and your heart to co-operate? Well, I hated what me and James were doing—in my head—but still, I couldn't seem to kick him out of my bed.

Lights fade.

SCENE ELEVEN

Lights up. JAMES *and* MEG *are alone now. He looks down at her on the bed, head covered by a pillow, and moves towards her helplessly. How to explain the unjustifiable? He doesn't know how he'll do it, all he knows is he* has *to do it, or he'll lose her.*

JAMES: I'm so sorry I lied… I panicked, Meg… I love you so much and I was scared I'd lose you…
MEG: [*from under the pillow*] That's not good enough.
JAMES: [*ashamed*] I know…

He waits for another reaction, but nothing comes. He moves closer to the bed.

I just… I can't tell you how sorry I am… I never meant for this to happen.
MEG: [*emerging from behind the pillow*] Oh, so it was an accident?
JAMES: [*grabbing at this*] Well, yeah. In a way it was.
MEG: What? Your zip fell open and gravity got the better of Naomi's undies and you tripped and fell inside her?

There's no answer to that. JAMES *ploughs on.*

JAMES: It was that weekend you went to the Jazz Festival. I was out with—
MEG: [*interrupting*] In Wangaratta? But that was *five months ago…*

An intensely awkward silence as JAMES' *squirming nod confirms this.*

JAMES: Yeah… I went for a drink with Tom, and we got talking to Naomi and a friend of hers. I didn't even know she knew you—

The second this is out, JAMES *realises what a misjudged excuse it is.* MEG*'s icy stare confirms it. He quickly tries to dig himself out of the hole that keeps deepening.*

[*Hastily*] Anyway—I was having a shit of a time at work—that was when the merger thing was going on, remember? And you'd been so busy at the office with Rachel, and planning the wedding with your mum—

MEG: [*interrupting, defensive*] I was training Rache up. I couldn't leave the poor girl in the lurch—

JAMES: I know that—

MEG: [*right over him*] And a wedding's a huge thing to organise—do you think it just magically happens?

JAMES: Of course not— But… you were so caught up in all of that stuff, and then you told me you were going away—

MEG: But I had to go. That Festival's one of my biggest clients!

JAMES: I know. I know all of that, Meg, but… I was kind of feeling invisible.

MEG: [*with a flash of fury*] So it's *my* fault *you* fucked someone else?

JAMES: No, no, of course not. That's not what I'm saying.

MEG: Just as well. Keep going.

JAMES: Well, like I said, I was missing you and—

But in spite of herself, MEG*'s feeling guilty.*

MEG: [*interjecting, guiltily*] It was one weekend—

JAMES: [*overlapping*] —and I got a bit pissed, and then we went to another bar with Naomi and her girlfriend and we had a few more—

MEG: [*interrupting coldly*] Which bar?

JAMES: [*thrown*] What?

MEG: Which bar did you go to?

JAMES: Does it matter? The Toff in Town.

MEG: You never take *me* to The Toff in Town.

JAMES: [*embarrassed*] I didn't *take* her, we just ended up there. Anyway… [*Struggling to continue*] We had some more drinks, and it got late, and then me and Naomi shared a taxi… and somehow we ended up at her place—

MEG: Somehow?

JAMES: Yeah. I wasn't thinking straight, Meg. I know that's not much of an excuse but… anyway, we went upstairs and… next thing I knew… well, we started—

MEG *interrupts, hands over her ears.*

MEG: Stop! Don't tell me anymore.
JAMES: Okay, fine.
MEG: No, tell me.
JAMES: Are you sure?
MEG: [*nodding, wincing*] Yes. I want to know.
JAMES: You don't look like you want to know.
MEG: No, I do want to know. Tell me.

Another beat of silence. JAMES *looks uncertain about whether to continue.*

Go on. Go.

JAMES: [*deeply uncomfortable*] Well, I was drunk, I was missing you, it was out of my control, Meg—and before I knew it we were—
MEG: [*interrupting*] Stop!

JAMES *stops, relieved, then almost straight away…*

No, go on. No, go.

JAMES: [*he hates saying this*] Well, we ended up in bed.

MEG *visibly winces.* JAMES *tries to touch her hand. She pulls away sharply.*

But it didn't mean anything. I woke up the next morning and I hated myself. I loved *you*—

MEG: [*overlapping*] You woke up? So you stayed the night?
JAMES: [*oops*] Well, yeah—but only because I was too drunk to—
MEG: [*interrupting*] And did you do it again in the morning?
JAMES: No! No way! I couldn't get out of there fast enough. And all I could think about all weekend was seeing you again.
MEG: [*remembering*] You surprised me with flowers… And I thought it was just because you loved me…
JAMES: It was. [*Beat.*] Mostly.

A small silence.

MEG: Alright, that might explain once, but Naomi said you were having an affair.

JAMES: Well, yeah, we were… sort of…
MEG: Sort of? What—you were *sort of* having sex on a regular basis?
JAMES: I know how it sounds, but it wasn't like that—
MEG: Oh, give me a break.
JAMES: [*overlapping*] After it happened the first time, I put it out of my mind. It was a one-off as far as I was concerned—but then Naomi started ringing me at work—and she turned up one day and asked if I could go for coffee. She'd just broken up with her boyfriend. I felt sorry for her.
MEG: So you screwed her as an act of charity? What a great guy.
JAMES: That's not what I'm saying. I just… I didn't know how to get out of it… And I didn't want to hurt her feelings.
MEG: Hers? What about *mine*…?

Her anger evaporates into tears.

JAMES: [*sincerely*] See, this is why I didn't tell you… I couldn't bear to see you so hurt… And I thought it'd all just sort itself out.
MEG: How? How can something like this just sort itself out?
JAMES: [*knowing this is lame*] I don't know… I thought the honeymoon's for six weeks, she'll get over it while we're away…
MEG: If you really thought that, then you're a moron as well as a bastard. And you're a coward too.
JAMES: Fair enough. I don't blame you for thinking that. I'm just glad the truth's out.
MEG: Really?
JAMES: Yeah. I hate lying to you. It's been horrendous for me.
MEG: But somehow you've managed it. As recently as ten minutes ago.
JAMES: I'm sorry about that, I panicked—
MEG: [*overlapping*] How many times did you have sex?
JAMES: Meg… don't…
MEG: How many?
JAMES: [*after a beat*] Three or four.
MEG: Bullshit.
JAMES: Five or six. It doesn't matter, Meg. It didn't mean anything.
MEG: It looked like it meant something to her.
JAMES: She knew I loved you. She knew we were getting married—
MEG: [*overlapping*] She's sexier than me.
JAMES: What? No—!

MEG: [*cutting across him*] She's voluptuous, isn't she? Men love that.
JAMES: Meg, I love *you*—
MEG: [*overlapping*] But she's got curves in all the right places, and legs up to here— She's got a gorgeous body. Hasn't she?
JAMES: Why are you doing this to yourself?
MEG: Just answer the question. Hasn't she got a gorgeous body?

>JAMES *hesitates, then…*

JAMES: I think her body's average.
MEG: Then why did you sleep with her?

>*As* JAMES *searches for the right answer…*

Because you could. God, what is it with men? Don't you have any willpower, or principles?
JAMES: Come on… you're not going to start on that 'all men are bastards' stuff—?
MEG: No, not all men. Only you.

>JAMES *bites back a defensive response, then…*

JAMES: Meg, I want to marry you. Doesn't that count for anything?
MEG: [*genuinely trying to understand*] But… if you really want to be with me forever, why would you do something like this?
JAMES: *Because* I want to be with you forever. *Because* I take marriage so seriously. In a weird way, that's exactly why.
MEG: How do you work *that* out?
JAMES: Look, I want to wake up with you every morning for the rest of my life. I've got no doubts about that. None whatsoever. And that's a great thing to feel, but I'll be honest, Meg, on one level I think it's been scaring the shit out of me too.
MEG: But why?
JAMES: Because I'm staring down the barrel of the fact that I'll never see another woman naked.

>MEG *'s not sure how to react. He feels like a heel.*

Okay, that sounds terrible—but it's scary to love someone so much that you never want to be with anyone else—and so, I guess this… opportunity… came up unexpectedly… and I suppose it was a bit like, well, I'll say goodbye to singlehood with this final, stupid fling… And that's all it ever was, Meg, a fling.
MEG: But… I need to be the only one.

JAMES: You *are*. You're the only woman I've ever wanted to have my kids, and the only woman I'd choose to spend my life with. This... this stupid thing... it was just a mistake. It *never* changed how I feel about *you*.
MEG: But how can you say that? If I'm the only woman you want, you shouldn't *want* anyone else.
JAMES: Meg, you're my soul mate. That was just sex.
MEG: *Just* sex?
JAMES: Yes. Just sex. And we've got so much more than that.
MEG: But haven't we got *that*, too? Isn't our sex good enough for you?
JAMES: Of course it is! It's beautiful! *You're* beautiful. And I love you more than anything. But...

His voice trails off. MEG *misinterprets the pause.*

MEG: But you want to have sex with other people?
JAMES: No! That's not what I'm saying, but... it's just... if you want me to promise that I'll never find anyone else attractive, I can't do that—
MEG: I know. I know that. But—
JAMES: [*overlapping*] Can you promise me that you'll never be attracted to another man?
MEG: Of course not—
JAMES: And can you promise that you'll never be *tempted* to have an affair?
MEG: I can promise that I won't act on it.
JAMES: Can you? Can you really?
MEG: Yes, I can.
JAMES: [*lowering his voice*] Meg, even *Angela's* had an affair.
MEG: Ssssh! I wasn't supposed to tell you that!
JAMES: She can't hear us.

MEG *looks thoughtful, anxious, tied up in knots.*

MEG: I don't like the way this is heading... Finding other people attractive's one thing, but... I have to know you're faithful, James. I need you to *promise me* this won't happen again.

JAMES *sighs, thinks for a moment, then decides to be courageously honest—at great risk.*

JAMES: It would be so easy for me to say, 'I promise I'll be faithful forever, Meg'—but I've told you enough lies, and I don't want to do that anymore. I *can't* promise that I'll never do it again—

MEG *gasps: That's really painful.*

[*Gently*] But I *can* promise that I don't *intend* to ever do it again, and I'll try with all my heart *not* to do it, and I'll always remember how important this is to you, and try to put your feelings first… And I'm not going to ask *you* to promise *me* any more than that either, because… I know how these things can happen…

MEG *is quiet, confused. She has no idea how to react.*

I'm not saying it will happen—I really don't think so—but I won't risk lying to you again…

MEG *is silent. A beat or two, then…*

[*Tenderly, tentatively*] Meg…? What are you thinking…?
MEG: I just want you to be the same person you were yesterday.
JAMES: I am. I'm still me, Meg. We're still us.
MEG: [*dubiously*] Really?

JAMES *nods with complete sincerity. He gets down on one knee, taking* MEG'*s hands.*

JAMES: I'm deeply, deeply sorry. This is something that should never have happened, and lying when you asked me was unforgivable. I'll never, ever lie to you again. I promise you that with all my heart.

MEG *is silent for a long time.*

[*Nervously*] Meg…?
MEG: I don't know what to say…
JAMES: [*vulnerable*] Please, just say you'll give me another chance?

More silence, but MEG *looks like she may be softening.*

I know I probably don't deserve it, but I can't imagine life without you… [*Nervously*] Will you marry me, Meg?

He waits on tenterhooks as MEG *thinks for a long moment.*

MEG: I don't know…

It's not the answer that he was hoping for, but he nods, accepting it.

JAMES: I'll spend the rest of my life trying to make you happy, if you'll let me…

He waits but MEG *is silent. Then…*

MEG: [*not harshly*] I need you to go now…

He nods and reluctantly gets up and walks to the door, turning as he gets there.

JAMES: I love you.

MEG: I know you do.

JAMES *smiles sadly and exits.* MEG *is still for a moment, then turns and meets the audience's eyes. Lights start to fade as we move into...*

SCENE TWELVE

MEG *addresses the audience directly.*

MEG: I blame Mum for this. I learned denial from her. She's a fantastic teacher. She gave me detailed, intricate lessons without one spoken word passing between us—which was, of course, the entire point. [*Beat, then slightly defensively*] Oh, I'm not a fool. I've had a niggling feeling about James... but I pushed it down from my brain and through my chest—carefully avoiding the heart area—and I kept pushing it down through my stomach and even further down still, until it was in the soles of my feet and every step I took squashed it.

It wasn't that hard... I was busy with work, so I just kept walking faster and faster; so fast that no-one could tap me on the shoulder and force me to face the truth...

Who wants to know that the man they adore—the man they're about to commit their whole life to—has been having sex with somebody else? Who wants to put on this amazing, magical dress and then have to take it straight off again and zip it back up in its plastic? Who wants to be thirty-three years old—with a biological clock that ticks so loudly it keeps you awake at night—and back in the singles wilderness? Not me...

A beat or two. She sighs, then retreats back into flippancy.

This wasn't part of the fairytale. But hey, this is the real world, isn't it? And it turns out my Prince Charming's a toad. [*Deeply angry*] I hate him. And you know what? I hate the others too. I do. I hate Naomi for betraying me, I hate Lucy for telling me, I hate Ange for not telling me, I hate James for cheating on me, then lying about it, and most of all for being honest, and I hate Mum for—well, I just hate her. [*Beat.*] But I hate myself the most. I hate the fact that I'm so smart, but I chose to be so bloody stupid. And I hate that if I had the chance, I might even do it again… [*Beat.*] I just wish it was yesterday, you know? This hurts too much. James isn't who I thought he was. There are bits of him I didn't know about, bits that break my heart in half… Can I really learn to love those bits, too?

Lights fade as we move straight into…

SCENE THIRTEEN

MEG *wipes her eyes and blows her nose with an air of frenzied urgency. The clock's ticking. There's no time for contemplation and she feels compelled to make a quick decision. She starts fiddling frantically with her wedding dress as the door opens and* COLLEEN *enters with a tentative smile. She's nervous, uncertain.*

COLLEEN: Sweetheart? I just saw James leave. Is everything sorted out?
MEG: [*frenzied, fragile*] Yeah, it is.
COLLEEN: Are you sure?
MEG: Yeah. I'm sure.
COLLEEN: Really?
MEG: [*shortly*] I just said so, didn't I, Mum?
COLLEEN: [*happily, briskly*] Alright, then! Well, let's get moving. Now Angela's gone down to pick up the flowers, and your father and the photographer will be here any minute, so we'd better get you into your veil—

She starts walking briskly to the wardrobe and gets Meg's veil out. MEG *stays still as her mother unzips the veil from its cover.*

Come on, Sweetheart, quick sticks. [*Starting to take the veil out*] Look at this beautiful—Oh no!
MEG: What?!
COLLEEN: It's gone all limp—!
MEG: What do you mean?!
COLLEEN: [*fussing with the veil*] It's not as full as it was when we picked it up!
MEG: [*crumpling into tears*] Have I got a flat veil?

COLLEEN *quickly realises her mistake. She's determinedly chirpy.*

COLLEEN: No, no, no! It's lovely, it's perfect. No, looking at it again, I was wrong. It's just right. And all we have to do is fluff it up, anyway. Sweetheart, don't cry. You'll have red eyes at your wedding.

MEG: [*sniffling*] I've got some Visine.

> MEG *is wiping away her tears with her hands.* COLLEEN *grabs some toilet paper (still on the bed from stuffing the shoes) and wipes* MEG's *face, then holds it under her nose like she's a little girl.*

COLLEEN: Oh, Sweetheart, come on... the veil looks beautiful... [*Holding the toilet paper under* MEG's *nose*] Here. Blow...

> MEG *does so.* COLLEEN *wipes her nose.*

Good girl. [*She throws the toilet paper away.*] Now let's put this on... Alright?

MEG: [*nodding, sniffling*] Alright.

> MEG *still sniffles as* COLLEEN *places the veil on her head. It has no floral headpiece yet.*

COLLEEN: Sit still... Here we are... Ohh, lovely...

MEG: Does it look silly without the flowers?

> MEG *starts heading for the mirror on the other side of the room.* COLLEEN *follows, all hustle and bustle.*

COLLEEN: Angela will have the flowers up here any second— Oh, I keep forgetting to tell you—now, the disco man rang yesterday and said that Fido song you wanted would have to—

MEG: [*cutting across*] Dido.

COLLEEN: What?

MEG: Her name's Dido, not Fido.

COLLEEN: Alright, whatever you like. Anyway, he thought he'd play that song when you're all entering instead of after the speeches. I said I thought that'd be fine, but I'd have to check with you too, of course, so what do you— [think?]

> But MEG *can't take her mother's denial anymore. She snaps.*

MEG: [*interrupting*] How can you do this?

COLLEEN: What? Do what?

MEG: How can you just pretend that nothing's wrong? Didn't you *hear* what Naomi said?

COLLEEN: [*flustered*] Yes, Sweetheart, of course I heard...

MEG: James has been having an affair! Don't you even *care*?

> *Poor* COLLEEN *doesn't know what to do. She's just been trying to do the right thing.*

COLLEEN: Of course I care, but you just told me everything was sorted out and I didn't want to spoil your day—
MEG: No, Mum, you didn't want to spoil *your* day!
COLLEEN: Meg...
MEG: This whole thing's all about what *you* want, Mum. It's got nothing to do with me. All *I* have to do is turn up!

> COLLEEN *starts, looks deeply injured. Her thoughts fly swiftly back to her own wedding. She takes a moment, then takes* MEG*'s hands.*

COLLEEN: Oh, Sweetheart, I'm sorry... I didn't mean to take over...
MEG: [*sniffling*] I know how much you've been looking forward to this. I don't want to let you down...

> COLLEEN *pulls* MEG *into a hug.* MEG *cries on her mother's shoulder.* COLLEEN *strokes her. In spite of her wedding mania, the bottom line is, she loves* MEG *more.*

COLLEEN: Oh, Sweetheart, you wouldn't be letting me down... [*A few beats of silence.*] I was just trying to make things easier for everyone... and I did want your wedding day to be lovely, but I don't care about that if it's not what you want... I love you, Meg... I just want you to be happy... and if you think you should call it off, that's exactly what we'll do.
MEG: Do you mean that?
COLLEEN: Of course I do. If you don't want to marry James, I don't want you to either...

> MEG *smiles at her mother, filled with love. They go into a warm hug.* COLLEEN *strokes* MEG *maternally. A few seconds pass. Then* COLLEEN *can't resist looking at her watch.*

But you *will* need to make up your mind fairly quickly.

> *The door opens and* ANGELA *re-enters with the flowers. She looks uncertain. Is there going to be a wedding or isn't there?*

ANGELA: Ah, the flowers...?
COLLEEN: I'm not sure if we'll be needing them, Angela...
MEG: Yes, we will. We'll be needing them.
COLLEEN: Are you sure, Sweetheart?
MEG: Yeah, I *am* this time. I love him. I want to marry him.
COLLEEN: Are you certain about this?
MEG: [*nodding*] Positive.

ANGELA: You don't *have to* go through with it, Meg.

MEG: I know I don't have to, but I *want* to.

It's said with such certainty that COLLEEN *and* ANGELA *are completely convinced.*

COLLEEN: [*smiling*] Alright, then! [*Getting to her feet*] We'd better get that headpiece on in a hurry.

ANGELA *takes Meg's floral headpiece out of the box. Ad lib favourable reactions. Then they attach it (it's on a slide comb) to the front of Meg's veil.*

Just bend your head down for a moment, Meg, that's right… Now, Angela… just—gently—slide it into there… That's right… [*etc.*]

MEG: Has she gone?

ANGELA: Who?

MEG: You know who I mean. Has she gone?

ANGELA: [*nodding*] She's well and truly gone, Meg.

MEG: I just need to know she's not here.

COLLEEN: She's not here.

The phone rings. ANGELA *moves over to answer it while* COLLEEN *fluffs up Meg's veil.*

ANGELA: [*into the phone*] Hello? Oh, hi, Mr Bacon, yeah it's Angela. Great. Yeah, okay. We'll be right down. 'Bye. [*She hangs up.*] Your dad's here, and the photographer's setting up down in the courtyard.

They all start rushing even more. As COLLEEN *hurries to the cupboard to get her coat…*

COLLEEN: Good! Angela, could you grab Meg's bouquet—?

MEG: [*overlapping*] I've got to fix my make-up first! I look awful!

COLLEEN: You look beautiful!

MEG: I'm a mess, Mum! You two go first. [*As they hesitate*] Go on. Get the bridesmaid and the parents shots. I'll be down in a minute.

COLLEEN: Are you sure?

MEG: [*nodding, putting on a shoe*] I've got to find the Visine and put on my shoes—

Meanwhile ANGELA *has been pinning Colleen's corsage onto her coat. She pricks her.*

COLLEEN: Oww! You go, Angela. I don't want to leave Meg alone—

MEG: [*all smiles*] Mum, I'm fine, I'm great, I'm getting married in forty minutes and at this rate we're not going to make it to the church.
COLLEEN: [*thrilled*] Alright then! [*Fiddling with her hair in the mirror*] We'll see you downstairs—out in the courtyard—five minutes?
MEG: *Three* minutes. Oh, and you both look gorgeous.

>ANGELA *and* COLLEEN *smile at the compliment.*

ANGELA: So do you, Meg. You look beautiful.

>MEG *gives a hollow half-laugh. She feels anything but beautiful right now.*

MEG: Yeah, right…
COLLEEN: [*teary*] You *do*, Sweetheart. You look like an angel… [*Then suddenly bossy*] Come on, Angela, quickly!

>ANGELA *and* COLLEEN *exit.*

>*Left alone,* MEG *grabs a full champagne glass in a frenzy and drinks it all in one gulp. Then her eyes land on Naomi's dress. She picks it up and stalks into the bathroom. We hear the sound of the toilet flushing.*

>MEG *emerges from the bathroom and frantically searches for her wedding shoes. She hurriedly tries to put on the shoes, tripping over her heavy dress and having to try the delicate operation from several different angles. Her air of frenzied urgency only makes it more difficult. She then searches through her make-up bag for the eye drops, only to accidentally spill the bag's entire contents on the bed. She groans and anxiously rifles through the cosmetics to find the eye drops. She grabs them, perches on the edge of the bed and leans back, applying a few drops to each eye. It stings.*

MEG: Ouch… ooh…

>*She sits still, eyes closed, head tilted back, face pointing up towards the ceiling, waiting for the drops to take effect, as…*

>*The door opens and* LUCY *enters.*

>*She stops in surprise as she sees* MEG *sitting on the edge of the bed in her full bridal regalia. She's thinking about whether to turn and leave when…*

[*With her eyes closed*] I said I'd be down in a— [*Opening her eyes, she sees* LUCY.] Oh. It's you.

LUCY: I thought you'd be gone by now. I came to get my stuff. I'll go.
MEG: It's alright. You can get your stuff.

> LUCY *nods defiantly and starts walking across the room to the bathroom.*

[*Coldly*] And then go.
LUCY: Right.

> LUCY *goes into the bathroom to get her toiletries bag. Meanwhile,* MEG *starts applying make-up in a self-conscious frenzy. She's anxious to appear indifferent to* LUCY*'s presence, but her air of indifference is palpably manufactured.*

> LUCY *emerges from the bathroom with her stuff and walks all the way across the room to the door. She's about to leave, when…*

MEG: It was true, Lucy. What you said.
LUCY: I know. I'm sorry.

> MEG *gestures towards her bridal regalia.*

MEG: I s'pose you think I'm stupid?
LUCY: I don't know. What the hell would I know? I just wanted you to have all the information.
MEG: [*dryly*] Yeah, well, thanks for that.

> *An awkward silence. As* LUCY *hovers in the doorway, preparing to leave…*

You can… hang around for a few minutes if you want…
LUCY: Do you want me to?
MEG: Do *you* want to?
LUCY: It depends on what *you* want, Meg.
MEG: I would've thought it was pretty obvious that I don't know *what* the hell I want right now.
LUCY: Yeah… Fair enough…
MEG: You'll have to decide.
LUCY: Okay, then. I'll stay.

> MEG *is clearly pleased. She starts sliding to one side of the bed, moving her dress to make room for* LUCY. LUCY *smiles and comes to sit beside her. Silence for a moment, then…*

Can I help you with anything?

Then, in spite of the overwhelming awfulness of the situation, MEG *can't resist sharing something ironic with her best friend.*

MEG: You know, I asked Naomi Bartlett to take your place.

LUCY: What?!

MEG: [*nodding*] I asked her to be my bridesmaid.

LUCY: You didn't?!

MEG: Yes, I did.

> LUCY's *instant reaction is a grin. She quickly stifles it, feeling guilty. But* MEG *is grinning too. And she's starting to giggle, though her mirth has a manic edge.*

LUCY: You're kidding?!

MEG: [*giggling*] Can you believe it? She had the dress on when I found out…

LUCY: Oh, my God…

MEG: Mum even put toilet paper in the toes of your shoes…!

LUCY: [*laughing openly*] Oh, my God…!

MEG: [*laughing*] And when I found out, we took the dress off her and she had to leave in her undies…!

LUCY: Oh, Meg…!

MEG: [*giggling*] God, why am I laughing? I can't believe I'm laughing. I must be hysterical… [*Wiping tears of laughter away*] Shit. Now I've stuffed up my make-up again…

LUCY: [*tentatively*] Do you want me to fix it?

MEG: Yeah, okay.

> LUCY *comes over and starts doing* MEG's *make-up for her.*

[*Grinning*] You know the story… Slap it on three inches thick but make it look like I'm not wearing any.

LUCY: Don't talk. Your foundation will crack.

> *She applies powder foundation to* MEG's *face.*

Okay… Let's just smooth it in a bit…

> MEG *grabs* LUCY's *arm in a sudden, urgent action—*

MEG: Lucy, what am I going to do? Should I marry him?

LUCY: I don't know, Meg. Do you want to?

MEG: Yes. No. I don't know. [*Beat. She sighs.*] He said he can't promise me he'll never do it again. He can promise he'll try really hard, but he can't promise for certain that he won't.

LUCY: Well, at least he's respecting you enough to be honest.
MEG: Yeah, I guess we both know where we stand now... Mind you, I thought we did before...

Another silence. LUCY *touches her sympathetically.*

Lucy, do you think you could be faithful to one person for the rest of your life?
LUCY: I'm probably the wrong person to ask.
MEG: Probably.

They share a grin, then MEG*'s grin disappears as she grapples with reality again.*

God, I just—I want to marry him but I don't as well.

LUCY *knows instinctively that* MEG *needs her to take control.*

LUCY: Well, how about we finish this for starters, [*the make-up*] so you can keep your options open?
MEG: [*nodding*] Okay...

LUCY *gets two blushers out of Meg's make-up bag.*

LUCY: Now, what blusher would madam like to wear? Burnished Rose, or Sienna Sunset?
MEG: I told you I'm incapable of decisions right now.
LUCY: Okay. Sienna Sunset then—
MEG: [*overlapping, decisive*] No, Burnished Rose.
LUCY: [*grinning*] Right. Burnished Rose it is.

She starts to apply it to MEG*'s cheeks.*

MEG: And just a little bit. I don't want to look like a clown.
LUCY: Oh, really? You're such a killjoy.
MEG: [*dryly*] Ha. Look who's talking.

They grin at each other, LUCY *a little ruefully.*

LUCY: Guess I asked for that one, didn't I?

They smile at each other again, then MEG *suddenly feels a burst of emotion.*

MEG: But seriously, Luce... thanks for telling me... It took a lot of guts...
LUCY: Keep still. Do you want Burnished Rose all over your nose?

MEG *suddenly grabs* LUCY *and hugs her tight.* LUCY *hugs her back.*

MEG: You're such a good friend...
LUCY: So are you.

> *They're wrapped in each other's embrace for a moment, then, as they pull apart...*

Want to do it?

> MEG *laughs and playfully pushes her away.*

MEG: Shut up!

> *They both grin. Then, after another short silence...*

Who *did* you do it with, Lucy?
LUCY: If I told you, you wouldn't believe me.
MEG: Oh, come on. I'd believe *anything* from *you*. Who was it?
LUCY: You really want to know?
MEG: I'm *dying* to know.
LUCY: Are you sure?
MEG: Just tell me!
LUCY: [*grinning*] Naomi.
MEG: What?!
LUCY: [*laughing*] It was Naomi Bartlett.
MEG: Oh, my God!

> *She gapes at* LUCY. *Then they both fall about giggling and laughing.*

LUCY: She's *anybody's*.

THE END

IT'S MY PARTY
(And I'll Die If I Want To)

It's My Party (And I'll Die If I Want To) was first performed at La Mama Theatre, Carlton, in conjunction with the Melbourne Comedy Festival, on 31 March 1993 with the following cast:

RON PATTERSON	Jim Daly
MICHAEL PATTERSON	Leon Teague
DEBBIE PATTERSON	Helen Rollinson
KAREN PATTERSON	Sarah Walker
DAWN PATTERSON	Libby Stone
TED WILKINS	Adriano Cortese

Dramaturg / Director, Catherine Hill
Designer, Linley Kensitt
Lighting Designer, Andrew Livingston
Stage Manager, Stacey Moulday

CHARACTERS

RON PATTERSON, mid 60s, robust, decisive, patriarchal
DAWN PATTERSON, mid 60s, warm, lovable, surprisingly astute
MICHAEL PATTERSON, 38, tense, image-conscious, driven
DEBBIE PATTERSON, 36, creative, fun, vulnerable
KAREN PATTERSON, 26, spoilt, self-absorbed, petulant
TED WILKINS, 25, polite, personable, eager-to-please

ACT ONE

The stage is in darkness.

Through the blackness we hear the loud ticking of a clock.

A few seconds tick away. Then the ticking fades out as a spotlight comes up.

A man in his mid sixties, dressed in an old-fashioned but immaculately neat suit, stands in the spotlight beneath a round clock. The man is RON PATTERSON. *The clock is on the wall of his living room. It reads 8.34 p.m. The living room is a study in beige suburbia. On one end of a cabinet sits a sizeable and intricately-detailed model of the* HMS Bounty *that* RON *has laboured over for many hours. A projector screen stands against a wall and a laptop sits nearby. On the table are plates of party pies and Cheezels, cocktail frankfurts and pavlova.*

RON: [*addressing the audience*] Good evening. At ten twenty-three p.m. on [*three months prior to the performance date*] my doctor gave me three months to live. By my calculations, that leaves me with exactly… [*looking at the clock*] one hundred and eleven minutes. So Dawn's invited the kids around for party pies and pavlova.

   Fade to black.

   The clock ticks loudly for a few seconds. Lights up.

   DEBBIE *is sitting on the lounge flicking through Dawn's* Women's Weekly. *She's dressed in jeans and a stylish top and has an air of tight control. Her brother* MICHAEL *is hovering near the table. He wears an expensive suit.*

MICHAEL: Party pies? They've got to be kidding. [*He bites into one, then discards it with disgust and glances tensely at his watch.*] I'm due on a conference call. How long is this going to take?

DEBBIE: [*turning a page*] I don't know any more than you do, Michael.

MICHAEL: This is so typical. Isn't it? Isn't it?

   DEBBIE *doesn't respond.*

He clicks his fingers and we come running. No. No. He doesn't click *his*. That'd entail a bit of effort. He gets someone else to click theirs for him. Who rang you?

DEBBIE: Mum.
MICHAEL: [*overlapping, this proves his point*] That'd be right. And what did she say?
DEBBIE: [*not wanting to get drawn into this*] She said, 'Dad wants you at our place tonight. It's very important.'
MICHAEL: My PA told me.
DEBBIE: Your *PA?!*
MICHAEL: Well, admittedly Mum tried to get through a few times. But I've had a lot of meetings.
DEBBIE: Michael.
MICHAEL: I would have called her back. I was waiting for the London Exchange to close.
DEBBIE: [*shaking her head*] You're going to work yourself into an early grave. You know that, don't you?
MICHAEL: Deb. Don't start—
DEBBIE: [*overlapping*] Well, have you looked in a mirror lately? You look about fifty.
MICHAEL: I looked twenty years younger before I left the office. It's coming *home* that ages me.
DEBBIE: You let it get to you too much. Just… try thinking tranquil thoughts. And take a few deep breaths… from your diaphragm…

    MICHAEL*'s looking at her like she's gone mad.*

MICHAEL: Spare me the yoga lessons, Deb. You hate being here as much as I do.
DEBBIE: Not anymore. I'm completely relaxed.
MICHAEL: You're completely relaxed?
DEBBIE: [*nodding*] Coming home causes me no stress at all.
MICHAEL: May I remind you last time we were here I had to restrain you from braining Dad with *The Bounty*?
DEBBIE: I'd had a bad day.

    MICHAEL *looks unconvinced.*

Well, I've been giving this whole issue some serious thought… and the thing is… Dad's not going to change, so *I* am. Water off a duck's back, Michael. I'm not going to let him get to me anymore.
MICHAEL: [*scoffing*] Yeah, right.
DEBBIE: [*overlapping*] You're not going to drag me into this. Just because *you* don't have the nerve to tell them the truth—

MICHAEL: [*overlapping*] Debbie, not now. Please. I just—*not now*, alright?

DEBBIE *stops and looks at him more closely. His distress is genuine. Her tone becomes gentler.*

DEBBIE: What is it, Michael? What's wrong?

MICHAEL *sighs. He leans forward conspiratorially.*

MICHAEL: Do you remember last Christmas?

DEBBIE: What about it?

MICHAEL: Monique loaned Mum her silver salad servers.

DEBBIE: So…?

MICHAEL: So… she's coming round tomorrow to pick them up.

The way MICHAEL *delivers this, it is obviously highly significant.*

DEBBIE: Well. It had to happen. You couldn't keep them apart forever.

MICHAEL: You know what this means, don't you, Debbie? It means I have to tell them *tonight*.

DEBBIE *reacts excitedly. She leans forward, grabs* MICHAEL'S *hands.*

DEBBIE: You're *finally* going to tell them the truth?!

MICHAEL: Well. *Some* of it.

DEBBIE *abruptly drops his hands.*

DEBBIE: [*exasperated*] Michael!

MICHAEL *gestures: Don't hassle me. It's hard.*

Monique will tell them if you don't.

MICHAEL: She won't. She's too embarrassed.

DEBBIE: [*overlapping*] You're always complaining about living a lie. Here's your perfect chance to tell the truth.

MICHAEL: [*shaking his head*] The divorce is going to be enough of a shock… In thirty or forty years… when they've adjusted to that… I'll slip in the fact that I'm gay.

DEBBIE: You can't avoid it forever, Michael—

MICHAEL: [*overlapping*] It's not as easy as you think. If you had something this big to tell them—

DEBBIE: [*overlapping*] If I had something big to tell Mum and Dad that was sort of connected to a timeframe, and still could change, and they could affect that thing—whatever it was—then in that case I wouldn't tell them yet…

MICHAEL: [*overlapping*] What…?

DEBBIE: [*overlapping*] But if it was something they could never change, that they'd just have to learn to live with, I'd tell them.
MICHAEL: You'd tell them *tonight?*
DEBBIE: Definitely. Look, we all know Dad's got... certain faults, but do you honestly think he'd want you living a lie?
MICHAEL: Absolutely. Positively. Yes.
DEBBIE: You're right.
MICHAEL: He's a bigoted bastard.
DEBBIE: Then do it for your own peace of mind. You've been wanting to tell him for years, Michael.
MICHAEL: It's big. I have to work up to it.
DEBBIE: [*sighing*] So you keep telling me. But at this rate Dad's going to be six foot under before you find the nerve.
MICHAEL: I *will* tell him before he dies.
DEBBIE: [*sarcastic*] Fabulous. *When* before he dies?
MICHAEL: Let's not get too specific. Just before he dies, alright? I *promise* I will tell Dad I'm gay before he dies.
DEBBIE: Great. Tell him in twenty years then, Michael—but don't come round to my place anymore moaning about you and Andrew.

A pretty young woman of twenty-six enters. This is KAREN. *She carries a bunch of flowers and wears an engagement ring.*

KAREN: Who's Andrew?
MICHAEL/DEBBIE: Nobody. / Hi. Nobody.
KAREN: *Nobody?*
DEBBIE: Nice flowers, Karen.
KAREN: This is so typical. Every time I walk into a room you two stop talking.
MICHAEL: Do you know what tonight's all about?
KAREN: That's right, Michael. Change the subject.
DEBBIE: Why did we have to come over so quickly?
KAREN: You never tell *me* anything, so why should I tell you? [*Beat.*] Even if I did know.
MICHAEL: Ah. So you don't know either?
KAREN: All I know is Dad rang me and said—
MICHAEL: [*cutting across*] *Dad* rang you?

    KAREN *nods.*

When?

KAREN: Why—?
DEBBIE: *Mum* rang *us*.
MICHAEL: When did he ring you?
KAREN: I don't know… the other day—
DEBBIE: The other day?!
MICHAEL: My PA told me. At four o'clock this afternoon.
KAREN: Well, no wonder. You're always on your BlackBerry. Poor Dad probably— [tried to get through.]
MICHAEL: Poor Dad?
KAREN: Yes. Poor Dad probably tried to get through but…
DEBBIE: Karen. You are such a suck.
KAREN: You just hate me because I'm a size eight.

>*The sound of a man clearing his throat.* RON *and his wife* DAWN *are entering from the bedroom area.* DAWN *is wearing her best and most sombre frock. She is very emotional. She's also tipsy—a fact which should not be immediately evident to the kids.*

RON: Michael—
MICHAEL: Dad.
RON: Debbie—
DEBBIE: Dad.
RON: *Darling.*

>KAREN *moves quickly to her father.*

KAREN: There you are, Dad…

>*She gives him a kiss and hands* DAWN *the flowers as…*

MICHAEL/DEBBIE: Why did we have to come over? / What's so important—?
RON: [*interrupting*] Please, no interruptions. What I have to say is difficult enough. [*Gesturing imperiously*] Dawn.

>*She stands beside him. He pauses for effect.*

Three months ago, after suffering a series of symptoms I won't detail at this point, I sought medical advice. The news wasn't good. I was terminally ill. The long and the short of it is, I have one hundred and eight minutes left to live. Which is why you're here. I think that's all I need to say at this point.
MICHAEL/DEBBIE/KAREN: But hold on a minute— / How do you know that—? / What's wrong with—?

RON: [*interrupting imperiously*] Let's not make an issue out of this. The undertaker's arrangements are already made so you won't need to trouble yourself with those details. Your mother's put some bubbles in the fridge. I'll grab us a couple of bottles.

> RON *heads towards the kitchen.* KAREN *moves to follow him as* DEBBIE *and* MICHAEL *stare at* DAWN, *aghast.*

KAREN: But… Dad… what do you mean…? You're not really dying…?

> RON *has disappeared into the kitchen.*

DEBBIE: Is this some kind of horrible joke?
DAWN: Your father was given three months to live at ten twenty-three p.m.
MICHAEL: But that's insane!
DEBBIE: It doesn't work like that, Mum!
MICHAEL: Those timeframes are approximations! When a doctor says three months he means—
DAWN: All I know is what your father told me at lunchtime.

> *The kids look at her in shock.* KAREN *puts an arm around her.*

MICHAEL: He told you at lunchtime?

> DAWN *nods mournfully. She hiccups.*

Let me just get this completely straight: Dad told you at lunchtime today that he's going to die tonight?

> DAWN *nods again.* KAREN *strokes her arm.*

KAREN: Poor Mum. You've had to live with this all afternoon.
DAWN: He came in from the letterbox and said, 'Well, Dawnie, there'll be no more gas bills for *me*'. That was when he told me he's passing away at ten twenty-three…
DEBBIE: That's ridiculous! He can't say exactly when—
DAWN: You know what your father's like, Debbie. He calculates everything down to the last minute. Remember when we installed the new hot water system? Ron said it would last us nine years. And how long did it last? Nine years to the day…
DEBBIE: Mum. You can't compare a person's life to a hot water heater.
MICHAEL: This is insane. What's wrong with him? What's he got?
DAWN: Some sort of terminal illness.
MICHAEL: *Some sort* of terminal illness?!

DAWN: Michael, darling, why are you always so obsessed with detail? Your father's left a file that explains everything. We're allowed to open it at ten twenty-four.
MICHAEL: What if he doesn't die at ten twenty-three? I'm busy. I've got places to be. Are we supposed to hang around here and wait?
KAREN: Michael!
MICHAEL: Well, this whole conversation is ludicrous. Dad's not going to die!
DEBBIE: Michael's right. He's perfectly healthy—
KAREN: Why are you two always so selfish? It doesn't matter whether *we* believe it. Because Dad does. And so does Mum.
DAWN: Thank you, Darling. [*She turns to* MICHAEL *and* DEBBIE.] And I don't think it's too much to ask for a bit of respect and consideration. These are your father's last precious moments on Earth…
DEBBIE: Oh, I'm sorry, Mum… of course, whatever you say.
MICHAEL: Yeah, whatever you want, Mum. [*A horrible realisation hits him.*] Umm, so this means that even if we don't believe Dad's going to die tonight, we have to act as if he *is*?
DEBBIE: [*amused*] Exactly. Looks like tonight's the night for any *topics* that need to be canvassed before he carks it.

As MICHAEL *sinks low in his chair:*

KAREN: *Carks* it? Debbie, that's so disrespectful—
DAWN: [*hiccuping*] We've got an hour to make Dad happy before he has to leave us forever. So let's see those smiley faces. Come on.

    RON *emerges from the kitchen with two bottles of sparkling wine.*
    DAWN, MICHAEL, DEBBIE *and* KAREN *turn to him with unnaturally bright smiles.*

RON: Right. Let's crack open the— [bubbly.]

    He stops as he sees their pointed 'smiles'.

Lighten up. I'm not dead *yet*.
KAREN: Oh, Dad, you're being so brave about this…

    RON *throws his arm around* KAREN*'s shoulders and squeezes her.*
    DAWN *watches emotionally.*

DAWN: He's the bravest man in the world.

    She hiccups loudly. RON *looks at her disapprovingly.*

RON: Have you been into the bubbly already?
DAWN: I did make a little headstart.
RON: Christ. That's all we need. Your mother dancing the cancan on top of my coffin.
DAWN: I'd never do that, Ron. I can't cancan.

She laughs at her unintended pun.

Oh. Can't cancan! That's funny, isn't it?
MICHAEL: Yeah, Mum.
RON: Here. Get that into you, Debbie.
DEBBIE: No thanks, Dad. I'll stick with mineral water.
RON: You don't want to farewell your poor old father?
KAREN: Debbie— [don't be selfish.]
DAWN: It's not like you to knock back a drop, Sweetheart.
DEBBIE: I'm not feeling very well.
DAWN: Oh, you poor pumpkin.
DEBBIE: I'm fine, Mum. I just— [need a quiet night.]
DAWN: You do look a bit pale.
RON: She'll survive, Dawn. I just wish I could say the same for myself.

He sighs dramatically, coughs a little. DEBBIE *feels guilty. She takes a glass.*

DEBBIE: I'll have one glass, then.
KAREN: Just drink it and stop making such a fuss.

RON *suddenly notices there is an extra champagne glass. He frowns, remembering something.*

RON: [*to* MICHAEL] Where's Monique?
MICHAEL: She's at her— [Pilates class.]
DAWN: [*overriding him*] Monique's got ping-pong on Tuesdays.
MICHAEL: Pilates.
DAWN: I'm sorry, but I don't care what she calls it. I can't help feeling very hurt, Michael. I did ask especially for you both to be here.
MICHAEL: I know, Mum. I'm sorry—
DEBBIE: Maybe there's another reason. Michael? Is there another reason Monique couldn't make it…?
DAWN: [*getting teary*] I think she's shown us where her priorities lie. And with your poor father about to die—
RON: Put a lid on it, Dawn. I want to propose a toast. [*He clears his throat authoritatively and raises his glass.*] To the Patterson family.

IT'S MY PARTY (AND I'LL DIE IF I WANT TO) 107

ALL: The Patterson family.

They clink glasses and sip their cheap bubbly. MICHAEL *spits his out.*

RON: I know I haven't always been the best father in the world—
KAREN: Yes you have!
DEBBIE: [*mimicking her*] Oh, yes you have!

MICHAEL *laughs.*

KAREN: Did you see that, Dad? Debbie and Michael are picking on me.
RON: Oh, Sweetie…
KAREN: They do it all the time. They call me a suck.
RON: That's bloody ridiculous.
KAREN: I'm not a suck, am I?
RON: Of course you're not.
KAREN: Oh, Dad, you're so awesome.

RON *glows. He gives* KAREN *a hug, oblivious to everything and everyone else.*

DAWN: [*indicating* DEBBIE *and* MICHAEL] Ron…
RON: Ah, anyway. As I was saying, running the stationery store took a lot of my time and energy, especially after bloody Officeworks opened around the corner and I had to pursue aggressive sales strategies and extend my opening hours… [*Fighting off the stressful memory*] Anyway… I was very busy for a lot of years of your lives, and maybe I didn't give you enough of my time and attention. [*A little emotional*] I hope you can all forgive me for that.
DEBBIE/MICHAEL/KAREN: Of course! / Dad… / Don't be silly.
RON: But luckily I'm a great believer in quality versus quantity. So I plan to spend the next… [*looking at the clock*] hour and thirty-seven minutes making up for any past mistakes by giving you my undivided attention.

MICHAEL, DEBBIE *and* KAREN *are deeply touched.*

With that in mind…

He gets a clipboard out of the cabinet and pieces of paper.

… I've prepared a schedule of events for the evening. You'll find them colour-coded for ready reference. Please take a copy and pass them along to the person next to you.

He hands out copies of the schedule to his bemused family as we…

Fade to black. The loud ticking of the clock.

A neatly-prepared PowerPoint slide is projected onto the screen on the wall. It reads: 'Item No. 1: A Family Prayer'.

Lights up. The ticking stops.

The family now kneels in an awkward circle, hands joined. A silence.
DAWN *gives* MICHAEL *a stern look.*

DAWN: Michael. We're waiting.

DAWN *hiccups.*

MICHAEL: I don't know what to say.

KAREN: Just say anything that comes into your mind.

MICHAEL: Dear...

DEBBIE: God.

MICHAEL: Thanks, Debbie. Dear *God*. Please bless the party pies and pavlova we are about to share and bless our husband and father Ron as he prepares to—

His BlackBerry starts ringing inside his suit jacket. He drops DAWN*'s hand.*

Jesus! I forgot my conference call.

DAWN: [*blasphemy*] Michael!

MICHAEL: Excuse me. [*He answers his BlackBerry.*] Yeah, Phil—are we ready to go? Why not? I know it's 6.30 a.m. in Boston—*you* should too. [*Putting his hand over the receiver*] This'll only take a minute. [*Back on the BlackBerry*] Is everyone else on the line? San Francisco? Dubai? London? Call him at home and get him out of bed *now*. I don't give a flying— [*He stops himself.*] Tell him whatever you like, Phil, this is *your* stuff-up. [*etc.*]

MICHAEL *is engrossed in his conversation and shows no signs of winding it up.*

DAWN: Maybe I should finish.

DAWN *and* DEBBIE *join hands over* MICHAEL*'s head. They bow heads again.* MICHAEL *doesn't even notice.*

Dear God. Please send down your bountiful blessings on your humble but worthy son Ronald Reginald Patterson as he prepares to depart this life—

IT'S MY PARTY (AND I'LL DIE IF I WANT TO) 109

MICHAEL: [*waving distractedly*] Ssssh!

    KAREN *starts crying during the final moments of* DAWN*'s prayer.*

DAWN: Please grant him a safe journey into the next life and send his soul flying heavenwards like a white dove in the endless blue sky. We pray that his spirit will be soaring high above the clouds though his body may be covered by mounds of hard dirt, buried six feet below the earth in a coff—

RON: Alright, alright. We get the picture. Your mother's a two-pot screamer.

    A giggling DAWN *sips her champagne again.*

MICHAEL: [*into his BlackBerry*] I'm not interested in excuses, Mate, just get onto Boston and get him on board—we need all our ducks in a row. [*He hangs up.*] Sorry about that. Where was I?

    He grabs a couple of hands indiscriminately.

Dear God. Please bless—

KAREN: [*interrupting disapprovingly*] We've finished, Michael.

MICHAEL: Oh. Ah. [*Making a mangled and circular Sign of the Cross*] Amen.

    Fade to black. The loud ticking of the clock.

    A new slide appears on the screen. It reads: 'Item No. 2: Unresolved Family Issues'.

    Lights up. The loud ticking stops.

    The family is now sitting at the table which is positioned lengthways away from the audience. RON *sits facing the audience. The clock is on the wall directly behind him.* MICHAEL *and* DEBBIE *sit on one side,* DAWN *and* KAREN *on the other.*

RON: What I'd like to do now is discuss with you kids as a group how you feel I've managed as a father. If you've got any queries or unresolved issues, I'd like to hear them. Any gripes you have with me at all.

    DEBBIE *and* MICHAEL *are filled with fire. At last, here's the chance to vent their spleens.*

DEBBIE/MICHAEL: Well, since you're asking— / As a matter of fact, I—

RON: [*interrupting*] You know, you do your best to put a roof over your kids' heads, sacrifice your dreams for theirs, and try and save enough of yourself to be there when they've got a problem. And then suddenly one day you're staring death in the face, and you have to wonder if that was enough. Who knows? Anyway. You were saying?

The kids recognise this emotional blackmail for what it is, but it works regardless. Their backdown is grudging.

DEBBIE/MICHAEL: Nothing.

RON: You were going to say something.

KAREN *gives* DEBBIE *and* MICHAEL *a look: Don't you dare.*

DEBBIE/MICHAEL: No we weren't. / No complaints, Dad.

RON: *No* complaints? Guess I'm not such a bad bloke after all…

RON'*s thrilled he got out of this so easily. But* DAWN *wants to get things out in the open, for everybody's sake.*

DAWN: Ron, I think there probably are some— [complaints.]

RON: [*interrupting briskly*] Right. Let's move straight onto the next item then! Private Moments with Michael.

MICHAEL: [*in a panic*] Ah. How long are these Private Moments going to be?

RON: Time's not exactly on our side, but they'll be long enough to resolve any long-term hostility and reach a greater depth of understanding for each other. Around four to five minutes, depending.

MICHAEL: Depending on what?

RON: On if we run overtime on other scheduled events.

MICHAEL *anxiously peruses his copy of the agenda.*

MICHAEL: Let me just get something straight. Debbie's Private Moments are up second last. So if everything else takes longer than expected, does that mean you might not talk to her alone?

RON: I'm hoping that she won't miss out, but yes, that may be the case.

MICHAEL: Can I swap my Private Moments with yours?

DAWN: Now, Michael. Your father made the schedule the way he thinks best. And I think we should respect his wishes, don't you?

MICHAEL: Yes, Mum.

MICHAEL *smiles weakly at* DEBBIE. *She grimaces: Good luck!*

Fade to black. The loud ticking of the clock.

Another neatly-typed slide is projected onto the screen. It reads: 'Item No. 3: Private Moments—Michael'.

Lights up. The loud ticking stops.

IT'S MY PARTY (AND I'LL DIE IF I WANT TO)   111

MICHAEL *and* RON *are now alone in the living room.* MICHAEL *smiles awkwardly.* RON *makes a gesture: Follow me. He leads the way to the sideboard and picks up a trophy.*

RON: You know how proud I was when you won this?
MICHAEL: That's a netball trophy. [*Pointing*] I won the spoon. Most Consistent at soccer.
RON: [*picking up a tiny teaspoon*] Of course you did. And I felt as if my heart was going to burst that day. But I have to tell you, Michael, that's nothing compared to the pride I feel right now.
MICHAEL: Dad—
RON: [*interrupting*] The father/son bond is a very special thing. We're the same man, a generation apart. But while we're the same we're very different too. Would you agree with that?
MICHAEL: Definitely. And that's why—
RON: [*interrupting*] So tell me about yourself, Mate. Tell me about Michael Patterson the man. I want to know what makes you tick.
MICHAEL: I'm glad you feel that way, Dad, because there *is* something I want to tell you. This is… it's really important to me. And I feel—very strongly—that I should take this opportunity to be completely honest with you…
RON: I'm all ears, Mate.

   MICHAEL *clears his throat nervously.*

MICHAEL: Hhhmmm… the thing is, Dad, what I'm about to tell you might come as a… well, it might not—no, it *will definitely* come as a shock to you. And…
RON: I don't think there's much that can surprise a man of my age.
MICHAEL: You'd be surprised.

   MICHAEL *pauses, trying to find the courage and the words. A long silence.* RON *fidgets a little.*

RON: Come on. What's on your mind, Mate? Get it off your chest.
MICHAEL: Well. It's… ah… it's about me and Monique…

   RON *nudges* MICHAEL *in a matey fashion.*

RON: She's bloody beautiful, Son!
MICHAEL: Yeah, Dad, she is, but in spite of that…
RON: You don't have to say another word. Your mother might get stroppy with Monique now and then, but she was your choice, and *I* respect that.

MICHAEL: And I appreciate you respecting that—but what I'm trying to say is that… ah… Monique can't give me everything I… The thing is… ah, sexually…
RON: [*winking*] I know what you're saying, Son. When I see a pair of beautiful tits walk past! [*Shaking his head*] There's a lot of temptations.
MICHAEL: There are other temptations too, Dad. And that's what I'd like to talk about— [now.]
RON: Kids'll fix it.
MICHAEL: What?
RON: You and Monique need to start a family. That'll get your mind off the skirts. Your mother'd love to be a grandma too. It'd give her something to focus on after I'm— [gone.]
MICHAEL: Dad. Listen to me. Just for a second. [*Beat.*] I'm attracted to people who resemble myself.
RON: You've got a healthy ego. That's no crime.
MICHAEL: No. What I meant was— [*His BlackBerry starts ringing.*] Damn. Excuse me. [*Answering*] Phil, did you get him? I don't give a shit if he's jogging on Boston Common—get him back *now*—you think we're the only ones who've done due diligence?! Are Dubai and London still waiting? Fuck! Well, tell them we'll re-schedule for thirty minutes—do I have to do *everything* myself?!

> MICHAEL *hangs up.* RON *smiles proudly.*

RON: That's the way, Son. If you're making friends, you're not making money.
MICHAEL: Dad. Please… just listen while I tell you about me and Monique…
RON: There's more?
MICHAEL: There's a lot more. It's… we're…

> MICHAEL *pauses again.* RON *is getting impatient. He looks over his shoulder at the clock.*

RON: You'll have to make it snappy if we want to stay on schedule.
MICHAEL: Well, I recently told her I'm… [gay] and so we decided to… [separate] and now she's… [moving out.]
RON: You sly bugger! She's already pregnant!

> MICHAEL *can't be bothered arguing. He smiles miserably as* RON *enthusiastically shakes his hand.*

Congratulations!

MICHAEL: Thanks, Dad.

Fade to black. The loud ticking of the clock.

Another neatly-typed slide is projected onto the screen. It reads: 'Item No. 4: Discussion of Upcoming Family Events Ron Won't Be Attending For Obvious Reasons'.

Lights up. The loud ticking stops.

The entire family is once again gathered in the living room. DEBBIE *is trying to catch* MICHAEL's *eye, but he won't look at her.* RON *is irritated by not having* DEBBIE's *attention. From now on* MICHAEL's *tension is far more overt.*

RON: Deb…? Deb…? Deborah. Front and centre, thank you. [*He pats the chair beside him.*] Dawn.

DEBBIE *is forced to sit down.* RON *ticks off the prayer and the Private Moments with Michael on his clipboard.*

Item Number Four: Discussion of upcoming family events that Ron—i.e. me—won't be attending… for obvious reasons.

KAREN *sniffles sadly. But* RON *is still quite excited by what he's just 'learned'.*

I think we should start this item with some news from Michael and Monique.

DEBBIE: [*to* MICHAEL] You *did* tell him?

RON *winks at* MICHAEL. MICHAEL *sits in sullen silence.*

RON: He did. And I'm proud of him.
DEBBIE: Ffff—God!
KAREN: What did he tell you?
RON: Michael? Why don't you share it with your mother and sisters?
DAWN: What is it, Sweetheart?
DEBBIE: I've got to say, Dad, I'm stunned. You're taking this incredibly well.
RON: It was a bolt from the blue, I admit, but—
KAREN: What is it, Michael?
DAWN: Tell us, Darling!
RON: Come on, Mate. Spill the beans.
MICHAEL: Well… it's… ah…

RON: Oh, stop fartarsing around, Son. Michael and Monique are having a baby!

DAWN: Oh, Michael, Sweetheart! I'm going to be a grandma!

KAREN: That's awesome, Michael. Congratulations!

DEBBIE: [*amused*] Yeah. Congratulations.

KAREN: [*to* DEBBIE] How come he told you but he didn't tell me?

DAWN: Oh, I've always loved Monique! How many weeks is she? Michael? Darling?

RON: Now I don't want you on Michael's back, Dawn. He's chosen to keep it a secret this long—

KAREN: He told Debbie.

RON: I'm sure he had his reasons for that. But when it comes to the crunch this is a private matter between Michael and Monique. [*Winking*] Isn't that right, Son?

MICHAEL: Let's talk about other upcoming events. There must be something more important than this.

DAWN: What's more important than our very first grandchild?

RON: A brand new Patterson! Let's drink to the little bloke, eh?

KAREN: Doesn't anyone care about my wedding? I thought *that* was an important upcoming event.

MICHAEL: Yeah, Dad! Let's talk about Karen's wedding!

KAREN: You don't have to if you're not interested.

RON: Of course I'm interested! I want to hear all about it. What are you wearing?

KAREN: Strapless Italian silk with a full skirt and a beaded bodice, and my veil will be attached to my bun.

RON: [*surprised*] Attached to your bum?

KAREN: [*peeved*] No, to my *bun*! My *hair*, Dad—I'm wearing it up.

RON: [*relieved*] Oh. Right.

DAWN: And Ben and his groomsmen are wearing black tails.

KAREN: Mum, I told you I don't like tails.

DAWN: But they look so smart, Karen.

KAREN: No they don't. They look try-hard.

DAWN: Well, I don't think so. But what would I know? I'm only the bride's mother.

KAREN: Debbie. Don't tails look try-hard?

DEBBIE: They *can*, yeah. But not always. Sometimes—

KAREN: Oh, forget it. Why am I asking *you?* She won't even be my bridesmaid.

RON: Why not?

DEBBIE: Karen, you know I'd love to stand beside you on your wedding day. But you're having pale pink with tulle petticoats. I'm thirty-six years old. I can't wear pale pink with layers of tulle. I'd look like one of those dolls on top of a toilet roll.

DAWN: I think you'd look lovely.

DEBBIE: You know I'll do anything else to make the day special for you, but—

KAREN: I'm sorry *you* haven't found a husband. Alright?

DEBBIE: What?

KAREN: I'm sorry you're ten years older than me and you still haven't found someone to marry you. But I don't see why you should take it out on me.

DEBBIE: Oh, grow up, Karen!

KAREN: Well, you're jealous, aren't you? I'm not saying I blame you. I would be too if I was you. But I don't see why that means you can't co-operate with my wedding.

RON: Your little sister's got a good point, Debbie. We all feel for you in your situation, but you have to be big enough not to let your jealousy spoil the best day of Karen's life.

DEBBIE: I am *not* jealous! I'm very happy for Karen! [*Beat.*] Mu-u-u-u-m!

DAWN: I know you're happy for your sister Debbie, but I think being a bridesmaid would be a nice way to show it.

    DEBBIE *takes a few deep breaths, trying to calm down.*

DEBBIE: Look. I'd rather not get tense or agitated right now. So could we please talk about something else?

KAREN: Alright. Whatever you say. Let's just pretend my wedding's not even happening.

DEBBIE: Oh, please. [*Sighing*] Look. Michael… help me out here.

MICHAEL: [*terse*] She doesn't want to be a bridesmaid because she'll look stupid in the dress.

RON: Maybe if she wore dresses a bit more often she wouldn't be alone in the first place. [*Beat.*] Men like to see a girl in a dress. There's nothing sexier than sneaking a peak at a pretty ankle. Isn't that right, Michael?

MICHAEL *grunts non-committally.*
You never know. You might even meet a nice bloke at the wedding.
DAWN: Now there's a thought. Karen, are there any nice single men coming for Debbie?
KAREN: I don't think I know any old enough.
DEBBIE: Look. I appreciate everybody's concern, really. But I'm fine. I've got a great life. I've got a wonderful job, lots of loyal friends, a… [*unable to think of a complimentary adjective*] family. I can afford to go places and pursue my interests. I'm blessed. And I just happen to be single. So what?
RON: [*sighing*] I just worry about you growing old alone.
DEBBIE: I'm not going to grow old alone.
KAREN: That's right, Dad. She'll have my children to play with.
RON: That's a thoughtful offer, Sweetie. Debbie, you should take your little sister up on that.
DEBBIE: [*through gritted teeth*] I will.
RON: Good. You'll make a wonderful aunty one day. [*Beat.*] And in the meantime I think you should get yourself a cat.
DEBBIE: Could we *please* get back to the tails?
DAWN: Oh. Well, I think morning suits are lovely, but—
RON: Dawn. Your day's long gone, Woman. Karen knows better.
KAREN: Mum's got a right to an opinion, Dad. If she likes them—
DAWN: But you *don't*, Sweetheart—
KAREN: But if you do—
DAWN: But it's your day, Karen. And if you feel that strongly—
KAREN: But you feel strongly too—
RON: [*interrupting*] This whole thing's shaping up to be a bloody bunfight. I'm glad I won't be around for it!
DAWN: Ron!
RON: I'm sorry, Sweetie. I suppose I'm just letting off some steam, because it breaks my heart to think of you walking up that aisle without me.
KAREN: [*a thought occuring*] Dad. If I can't walk up the aisle with you, I think… in spite of the tails situation… I'd like *Mum* to give me away.
DEBBIE: I think that's a great idea.
DAWN: Oh, Karen!
RON: Your *mother?*
KAREN: If Michael doesn't mind.

MICHAEL: Absolutely not.
KAREN: Mum?
DAWN: Oh, Sweetheart. I'd be the proudest woman in the world.
RON: I like this idea as much as anyone, but I have to ask whether it's appropriate.
DAWN/DEBBIE/MICHAEL/KAREN: What do you mean? / Why not? / What's wrong with it? [*etc.*]
RON: I've never seen a mother do it before.
KAREN: So? Just because you haven't seen it before…
RON: Have you, Dawn? Ever seen it?
DAWN: Well, no Ron, but…

> *Her voice trails off.*

DEBBIE: *I* have! Kristy's father lives overseas and *she* walked down the aisle with her mum—
MICHAEL: [*overlapping*] And so did Monique's cousin Julie—
DEBBIE: It's not unusual at all. It's quite common now—
RON: [*cutting across imperiously*] No! As much as I like the idea, it's a man's job. Michael should give Karen away.
MICHAEL: Karen wants Mum to do it.
DAWN: Do you really think it's inappropriate, Ron?
DEBBIE: Of course it's not inappropriate.
RON: [*to* DAWN] You'll be busy with flowers and what-not won't you?
KAREN: Dad, why are you trying to spoil it for Mum? She wants to do it. And *I* want her to, too.
RON: And you'll have your hostessing duties don't forget.
MICHAEL: Are you deaf as well as terminally diseased? Karen wants *Mum* to give her away!
DAWN: Michael! How can you talk to your poor father like that? The man's got an hour to live!
MICHAEL: I'm sorry, Mum, but I'm sick to death of the way he tries to manipulate— [things his way.]
RON: It's alright, Son. You don't have to explain. Anger is one of the five stages of grief. He seems to be making an early start.
DAWN: Oh, Sweetheart, I should have realised…
KAREN: So it's settled then. Mum's going to give me away. [*Beat.*] It is settled. Isn't it? Dad?

> RON *gives a little wheeze for effect.*

RON: Apparently.

DAWN: Oh, Ron... I wish you could be there to see it.

RON: Why can't I see it now? [*Beat.*] Let's have a trial run for your old Dad. So I can picture it, and pack it away in my mind to take up to... [*waving his hand vaguely in the air*] wherever I'm going, with me.

DAWN: Karen, Sweetheart?

KAREN: I don't think you'll get much of an idea.

RON: Any idea is better than nothing.

KAREN: I don't want to, Dad. Ben isn't here and I haven't got my dress and the bridesmaids aren't here and—

> RON *starts coughing.* KAREN *feels instantly obliged.*

Are you alright? Alright... I'll do it.

> RON *instantly 'recovers'. He briskly takes control, moving furniture to form a makeshift aisle.*

RON: Right. I'll make an aisle. [*To* KAREN] You go and pop your face on. [*Moving furniture*] Debbie. Make yourself useful. Michael, give me a hand, Mate.

> *The slightest hint of hesitation from the increasingly disgruntled* MICHAEL *and...*

Come on. On your bike, Mike.

> MICHAEL *grumpily helps* RON *as* DAWN *grabs* KAREN*'s arm.*

DAWN: Debbie. Can you get Grandma Hurley's lace tablecloth out of the linen cupboard, Sweetheart? I'd get it myself but I'm not sure I can walk that far.

> *She giggles in a tipsy manner.* RON *rolls his eyes.* KAREN *is getting a little tetchy.*

RON: Christ, Dawn. You're a bloody embarrassment.

KAREN: She's just having a good time, Dad.

DAWN: We're *all* having a good time, aren't we, Sweetheart?

> KAREN *is holding* DAWN *up. She almost trips.* RON *grunts disparagingly.* DEBBIE *brings the lace tablecloth over.*

DEBBIE: What do you want this for?

DAWN: I'm going to put it on Karen's head.

KAREN: What...? Mum...

DAWN: [*overlapping*] Come on, Sweetheart. Quick sticks.

> *She puts the lace tablecloth on* KAREN*'s head.* KAREN *is getting more irritated every second.* DEBBIE*'s laughing.*

Oh, lovely... Ron, look! She looks like an angel.

KAREN: I look like an *idiot*. [*She frowns as her eye catches something on the edge of the lace tablecloth.*] What's that?

DAWN: A chutney stain.

> DAWN *giggles drunkenly.*

KAREN: [*agitated*] Can we start now, please?

RON: I'm the minister. Michael, you're the congregation.

> *He gestures impatiently for the morose* MICHAEL *to stand up.* MICHAEL *ignores him.*

DEBBIE: What about me?

RON: You're the bridesmaid.

DEBBIE: Dad, weren't you listening to anything before? I'm not going to be— [a bridesmaid.]

> RON *coughs and wheezes some more.*

DAWN: Ron? Are you alright?

RON: I just wish people would be a bit more helpful...

KAREN: Don't worry about Debbie. She hates me. I'm used to it.

DEBBIE: I do not hate you.

KAREN: You do so. [*To* RON] She hates me!

RON: [*wheezing, to* DEBBIE] Are you happy now your sour grapes have ruined the best day of your sister's life?

> DEBBIE *almost loses her temper.*

DEBBIE: I *do not have sour*— [*She stops and controls herself.*] Alright, alright. If it means that much to everybody... I'll do it.

DAWN: Good girl. [*Pointing*] Use those flowers as your bouquet, Sweetheart.

> DEBBIE *takes the flowers that* KAREN *brought* DAWN *earlier in the evening and holds them as a bouquet, complete with vase.*

DEBBIE: Can we just get this over with?

KAREN: Let's just do it. Please?

DAWN: I think I'm going to cry!

RON: All rise.

> MICHAEL *ignores him.* RON *gets a little impatient.*

Congregation rise!

> MICHAEL *grumpily gets to his feet.*

I'll hum the music. Michael, you help. One-two-three—Da da da da! Da da da—

> MICHAEL *hums with a decided lack of enthusiasm.* DAWN *and* KAREN *start walking behind* DEBBIE. KAREN *is basically propping* DAWN *up.*

KAREN: Debbie! You're walking too fast!
DEBBIE: Sorry.

> DEBBIE *slows down dramatically.*

RON: Dawn! Stand up straight, Woman!
DAWN: I don't think I can.
DEBBIE: Is this slow— [enough?]
KAREN: [*interrupting*] Mum! Watch out!

> *But too late.* KAREN *and* DAWN *run up the back of* DEBBIE. *They all fall over.*

DAWN: [*giggling*] Ooops. We ran up Debbie's bottom.
DEBBIE: [*overlapping*] Are you okay, Mum?
KAREN: [*overlapping*] When I said slow down I didn't mean stop.
DEBBIE: I didn't stop.
MICHAEL: [*picking* DAWN *up*] Mum… are you alright?
DAWN: [*overlapping*] I feel all wobbly.
RON: No bloody wonder. Sit down and stay out of mischief. Michael. You're taking over.
MICHAEL: No I'm not.

> RON *starts coughing and wheezing again.*

RON: I want to see you walk your sister up the aisle.
MICHAEL: Karen wants *Mum* to walk her up the aisle.

> *A beat as* RON *wheezes with conviction.*

Are you okay?
DAWN: Ron? Are you alright, Darling?

IT'S MY PARTY (AND I'LL DIE IF I WANT TO)

KAREN: You should rest, Dad. And I don't like doing this anyway.

RON: [*coughing and wheezing*] I'd just love to see you all… one last time…

> RON*'s voice trails off as though he is too weak to speak further. They gather around him anxiously.*

MICHAEL: [*weakening*] Dad. Karen wants Mum to give her away.

KAREN: I don't want anyone to. Not today. I feel like we're making a mockery.

RON: [*wheezing, to* MICHAEL] Please? Can't I see you giving your sister away and Debbie being bridesmaid?

DEBBIE: I don't want to…

> RON *wheezes and doubles over as though in intense pain.* DAWN *rushes to his side.*

DAWN: [*her legs wobbly*] Ron! Darling! Are you alright?

RON: [*overlapping, coughing*] Is it too much for a dying man to ask?

> DEBBIE *and* MICHAEL *know that* RON *is manipulating them. But at the same time his wheezes are making them anxious. They exchange a look, intercepted by* KAREN.

KAREN: If you won't even do it when Dad's this sick—!

MICHAEL: You said *you* don't want to do it!

KAREN: I don't.

DEBBIE: Then Karen—

KAREN: [*interrupting*] But Dad wants to see it! And he's practically dead!

> RON *wheezes loudly. He coughs for additional impact.*

DAWN: Ron, darling! Please, Michael, Debbie?

MICHAEL: Okay. Of course.

DEBBIE: I'm sorry. We'll do it.

> *Instantly* RON*'s coughs and wheezes cease. He stands up straight. He takes control.*

RON: Michael. Take your sister's arm—

> RON *grabs* MICHAEL*'s arm and arranges it around* KAREN*'s arm.* MICHAEL *shrugs him off in irritation.*

MICHAEL: I know what to do, Dad.

RON: Debbie, you walk about two and half feet in front.

KAREN: [*to* MICHAEL] Is it that horrible to hold my hand for two seconds?

MICHAEL: Oh, what?
KAREN: You yanked your arm away like I stink!
MICHAEL: Karen—
DEBBIE: [*overlapping*] Can we just get this over with please?
KAREN: That's your whole attitude to my wedding, isn't it?
DEBBIE: *You're* the one who's been saying— [you didn't want to do this.]
RON: [*interrupting*] For Christ's sake, leave your little sister alone!
DEBBIE: What did I say?
RON: [*interrupting*] I'm fed up with you two picking on poor Karen.
MICHAEL: *Me?* What did *I* do?
RON: [*yelling*] You get down the other end of the room and give your bloody sister away!

> KAREN *furiously pulls the tablecloth off her head. She bursts into tears.*

KAREN: [*crying*] I don't want to do it anymore! I've got to get this tablecloth off—my—head! I just want to stop! Alright?!

> RON *makes his way over to* KAREN. *He puts his arms around her and fixes a furious glare on* DEBBIE *and* MICHAEL.

RON: It's okay, Sweetie, you don't have to do it. [*To* MICHAEL *and* DEBBIE] I hope you two are pleased with yourselves.

> *Fade to black. The loud ticking of the clock.*
>
> *Another neatly-typed slide is projected onto the screen. It reads: 'Item No. 5: Family Slides (In No Particular Order)'.*
>
> *The loud ticking stops but the lights remain off and Slide #1 appears, showing a smiling group of young parents and infant children around a Christmas tree.*
>
> RON *now stands behind the laptop.* DEBBIE, DAWN, MICHAEL *and* KAREN *are seated on chairs arranged in rows. The air is thick with tension.* KAREN *is openly crying.*

DEBBIE: What year was that?

> *Almost before her question is finished,* RON *rips the slide off.*

DAWN: 1979, when you were— [three.]

> RON *has whipped the slide away.*

Ron?

RON: Time's working against us. The wedding practice took longer than it would have if people had been more co-operative.

> RON *puts Slide #2 on. It's a group of people at a christening in the mid seventies. Ad lib sighs, reactions.*

That was… ah… someone's christening.
DAWN: [*full of emotion*] It was Debbie's.
DEBBIE: Mine? Which baby am I?
MICHAEL: [*grinning*] The fat one.
DAWN: [*overlapping*] You're the one in the middle, Sweetheart, see? And there's Michael standing next to Aunty Lorraine.

> DEBBIE *gets to her feet and moves closer to the slide to get a better look. She looks like a shadow puppet.*

DEBBIE: *Which* baby am I? [*Pointing*] This— [one?]

> RON *whips the slide away as* DEBBIE *stands looking at it.*

RON: We've got a lot of slides to get through. Sit down.

> RON *moves to Slide #3. It shows three happy young couples gathered around a Christmas tree. The reminiscence surrounding this slide is strictly between* RON *and* DAWN.

DAWN: Ah, there's the old gang…
RON: That would've been at Christmas drinks.
DAWN: [*overlapping*] Oh, remember those Christmases, Ron? We used to find mistletoe *everywhere!*
KAREN: [*sniffling sulkily*] How come *I'm* never in the family slides?

> RON *moves to Slide #4. It shows a woman and a group of kids sitting beside a snowman.*

RON: Here you are, Sweetie.
DAWN: With Mr Snowman.
KAREN: I remember that snowman! We made him with the Johnsons. But *I* put his buttons on, didn't I?
RON: [*overlapping*] That's right, Sweetie. I showed you how.
MICHAEL: No you didn't.
RON: Yes I did. And then I showed her how to make his hat.
MICHAEL: Me and Debbie made that snowman's hat.
RON: No. *I* showed Karen how to sculpt the snow and then—

MICHAEL: [*interrupting belligerently*] Debbie, didn't *we* make that snowman's hat?

DEBBIE: Yeah. Me and Michael made the hat.

MICHAEL: See, Dad? You're wrong!

RON: I paid for every one of those bloody holidays. I ought to know what went on.

MICHAEL: Yeah, well, that was the winter I was in Year Nine. And you weren't even there yet!

RON: [*not believing him*] I wasn't there? Then who took the photo?

DAWN: Uncle Barry did.

> RON *stops and stares at* DAWN *disparagingly.*

Umm… you *were* a bit late for that holiday, Ron. You hadn't actually arrived yet.

MICHAEL: See?!

RON: So *you* made the snowman's bloody hat. Let's not make an issue out of it.

> RON *moves between slides of the family on holidays with cousins and other relatives. He moves through them faster and faster as he looks towards the clock.*
>
> *Slide #5.*

DEBBIE: Oh, look. There's Cousin Louise. Is she still living in Wagga Wagga?

DAWN: Oh, yes. Three children now.

RON: *Three* kids. And she's only twenty-eight. Her parents are very proud.

> *Slide #6.*

KAREN: Whose party was that?

DAWN: It was Michael's sixth birthday. Look, Michael, there's Sally Smithkin in the little pink hat.

KAREN: [*peering at the slide*] Oh, she was cute…

RON: Sally was a good girl. Quiet and respectful. Michael could have had her if he wanted her.

MICHAEL: Dad.

KAREN: What's so great about being quiet and respectful?

RON: [*overlapping*] She had her eye on your big brother the whole time they were growing up. But Michael was too busy with all his other birds. Eh, Mate?

IT'S MY PARTY (AND I'LL DIE IF I WANT TO)

MICHAEL *grunts non-committally.*

She married another fella in the end. She was one girl who had no shortage of offers.

DEBBIE: [*a little touchy*] What's that supposed to mean?

RON: Nothing.

Slide #7.

DAWN: Oh, there you all are outside the tent—

Slide #8.

MICHAEL: And there's that canoe Jamie had. We pushed him out of it once and— [he fell into the water.]

Slide #9.

DEBBIE: Oh. I remember that teddy bear. It was my favourite. I used to— [take it everywhere.]

Slide #10.

DAWN: There's me and Dad on the toboggan! We beat— [Lorraine and Barry every race.]

Slide #11.

KAREN: Could you slow down a bit, Dad?

RON: We're way behind schedule.

KAREN: But—

Slide #12, Slide #13, Slide #14, Slide #15, Slide #16. Slide #14 shows Debbie dressed up for her Year Ten formal with a gangly-looking sixteen-year-old-boy.

DEBBIE: Stop for a second! Go back. Go back.

RON *goes back to Slide #14.*

[*Remembering fondly*] Look, me and Brad…

DAWN: Your first boyfriend ever. He was lovely.

MICHAEL: He was a loser.

RON: He'd be long married by now.

DEBBIE: [*bristling*] No, Dad, you're wrong. He never got married.

DAWN: Sweetheart! Really? You should ring him up—

DEBBIE: He lives with Caroline. They've got three kids.

RON: If they've got three kids, why aren't they married?

DEBBIE: I guess they chose not to formalise things.
DAWN: But that doesn't seem fair on the poor children—
DEBBIE: Mum. A lot of couples don't get married. They choose to raise their families in committed, lifelong de facto relationships—
RON: [*interrupting*] No, that's just a bloke trying to hedge his bets. If he loves a girl, he'll marry her.
DEBBIE: God, that is so archaic—
KAREN: It's true, Debbie.
RON: [*to* DEBBIE] I just hope that one day some bloke will realise how lovable *you* are.
DEBBIE: And until then I'll remain an embarrassment. Right?
RON: What are you on about?
DEBBIE: No, what are *you* on about? You act like being single is a *social disease*—are you living under a rock?
DAWN: Debbie!
DEBBIE: [*speaking over her*] Newsflash, Dad—it's 2011. Twenty-five per cent of all Australian households only contain one person.
DAWN: Oh, is that true? It's so sad…
DEBBIE: M-u-u-u-m!
RON: See? Your mother agrees. We don't like seeing you sad.
DEBBIE: I'm not sad! I love my life. [*Taking a deep breath*] I'm fine when I'm away from here—I couldn't care less about being single—but as soon as I walk in the front door I feel this huge *pressure*—
RON: [*interrupting*] That's all in your head.
DEBBIE: How can you say that? Whenever— [I come home…]
RON: [*interrupting*] Well, what's so bloody hard about it, for Christ's sake? You go out, you meet a man, you go to the movies, you get engaged. Everyone else can do it.

> DEBBIE *can't stand it any longer. She jumps to her feet and stands in front of the projector. She looks like a particularly aggressive shadow puppet.*

DEBBIE: [*interrupting, screaming*] It's your fault I'm still single! [*She advances towards him.*] It's *your* fault I always pick the wrong men!

> DAWN *stands up, another shadow puppet.*

DAWN: *Our* fault?!
DEBBIE: No! *His* fault!
RON: Why is it *my* fault?!

DEBBIE: Because you've always been… you're so… you're… *emotionally unavailable!*
RON: Emotionally what—?
DEBBIE: And now I end up with emotionally unavailable men!
DAWN: Now, Debbie, I don't think this is the time—
DEBBIE: I'm always trying to win their attention. Just like I'm always trying to win yours. And when I win it, it isn't worth it!
DAWN: Deborah—
DEBBIE: I've watched Dr Phil, Mum. I know how it works!
KAREN: For God's sake, Debbie. Don't you think this belongs in your Private Moments?
RON: It's alright, Sweetie. She's obviously quite upset. We can deviate from the agenda. Briefly.
DEBBIE: See?! See?!
RON: What? What?
DEBBIE: It's going to kill you to 'deviate from the agenda' to discuss something that means this much to me! I'm not Item Number Nine. I'm your *daughter!*
RON: Could we just tone down the hysteria a little—
DEBBIE: When we were kids you were always pre-occupied. Your mind was on stationery supplies or some other stupid thing. I remember when I was little, and I'd do a somersault. I'd say, 'Look Mum, look Dad. I can do a somersault!' And Mum would always look. From the start to the finish. But you only pretended. Because when I put my head up again you'd be looking somewhere else. And you'd turn back and say, 'That's was great, Debbie! Clever girl!' But you hadn't even been looking.
RON: So that's what this is all about? Because I didn't watch you do a somersault?
DEBBIE: Oh, what's the point?
MICHAEL: For once in your selfish life, Dad. Stop thinking about yourself for thirty seconds and *listen* to what Debbie's telling you.
DAWN: Michael!
RON: Well, alright then… do one now.
DEBBIE: What?
RON: Do a somersault now. [*He moves over and turns the light back on.*] Come on. Do a somersault for me.

> DEBBIE *looks nonplussed, to say the least.*

You've got my undivided attention.
DAWN: That's a nice idea, Sweetheart. Do a somersault for Dad.
DEBBIE: I can't do a somersault now.
DAWN: Of course you can.
RON: I'm waiting.
DAWN: Go on, Debbie. Your father's watching.
DEBBIE: Mum, I don't feel well. Remember?
RON: One small somersault won't hurt you.
DAWN: It'll be over in thirty seconds, Sweetheart, and think how happy you'll be that Dad is watching!
RON: You'll have my complete concentration.
DEBBIE: What's the point in me doing a somersault here? That's not the issue.
RON: I thought that was exactly the issue.
DAWN: Your father's trying to meet you halfway, Darling.

> DAWN *hiccups.* DEBBIE *looks helplessly to* MICHAEL *and* KAREN.

KAREN: [*impatient*] You're always saying Dad never pays attention.
DEBBIE: But this isn't going to— [change anything.]
KAREN: [*interrupting*] He's paying attention. What else do you want?
DAWN: Come on, Sweetheart. Time's against us.
MICHAEL: Just do it and get it over with.
DEBBIE: Michael!
DAWN: Come on, Debbie.
RON: I'm waiting.
MICHAEL: [*overlapping*] They won't get off your back till you do.
RON: I am not on Debbie's back. I'm simply demonstrating my interest in watching her do a somersault.
DEBBIE: This is ridiculous…
DAWN: [*overlapping*] Come on, Sweetheart.
KAREN: [*overlapping*] What's the problem *now?*
MICHAEL: [*overlapping*] Just do it.
RON: Tell you what—why don't I do a forward roll too? And you don't even have to watch me do mine.
DEBBIE: No, Dad. It's… alright. I'll do it.
DAWN: Good girl.

> DEBBIE *sighs and prepares for the feat.*

DEBBIE: I can't believe I'm doing this.
DAWN: We're all watching, Debbie.
RON: Especially me.

> RON *leans forward intently, self-consciously focusing all his attention on* DEBBIE. DEBBIE *bends herself at the knees, preparing.*

DAWN: Good luck.
KAREN: [*overlapping*] Hurry up.
DEBBIE: Here goes…

> *As* DEBBIE *starts to lean over she notices* RON *glancing furtively at the clock.*

He's looking at the clock!
RON: I am not.
DAWN: Come on, Sweetheart. Just do it.
MICHAEL: Go, Deb.

> DEBBIE *angrily throws her dignified thirty-six-year-old body into an undignified somersault on the floor. Halfway through she twists her back.*

DEBBIE: Oww!
RON: What's wrong?
DEBBIE: [*hunched over*] Oww!

> *Everyone rushes to help* DEBBIE. RON *and* DAWN *get there first. They help her up, physically supporting her. She's hunched over in pain.*

DAWN: What happened?
DEBBIE: [*grumpy*] My back!
RON: That was a terrific somersault, Sweetie. Spot-on.
DEBBIE: Shut up!

> *She stamps her foot, then squeals in pain. It hurt her back.*

DAWN: Debbie!
RON: What have I done now?
DEBBIE: It's your fault! Everything's your fault!
RON: *Everything's* my fault?
DEBBIE: Yes!
RON: Well, thank Christ for that. Now we know why the world's going wrong. It's *my* fault about the Global Financial Crisis, it's *my* fault the Tigers are playing like kittens, it's *my* fault you're still single.

DEBBIE: Yes! Yes! Yes!
RON: Far be it from me to bring some icy-cold logic to this, but Michael and Karen had the same father as you. And Karen's getting married.
DEBBIE: Really? Nobody mentioned that.
KAREN: You hear how mean she is to me, Dad? She hates me.
DAWN: Now, Debbie, it's not Karen's fault.
DEBBIE: Well, I'm not Karen and she's not me—
KAREN: [*overlapping*] Thank goodness!
DEBBIE: [*overlapping*] Besides, by the time Karen came along you were more interested.
RON: But what about Michael? He was born before you were, and he found Monique.
MICHAEL: Monique and me aren't a good example to use—
RON: Of course you are. That girl worships the ground you walk on. You've been married nine years—
MICHAEL: [*overlapping*] She hates me, Dad. We're getting a divorce.
DAWN: What?!
MICHAEL: There. I said it. We're getting a divorce.
KAREN: You're getting divorced?!
RON: Why didn't you tell us?
MICHAEL: It's a mutual thing.
DAWN: Oh, Michael—what's happened, Darling? Has she met someone else?
MICHAEL: No, Mum. *I've* met someone else.
RON: *You've* met someone else?

    MICHAEL *nods.*

KAREN: You're leaving Monique for someone else?

    MICHAEL *nods again.*

RON: Well. Who is she?

    MICHAEL *is silent.*

DAWN: Who's this girl who's stolen your heart?
RON: Come on, Son. What's her name?

    The briefest hesitation before MICHAEL *says…*

MICHAEL: Andrew.

    A long silence.

DAWN: Did you say… *Andrea?*
MICHAEL: No, Mum. I said Andrew. [*Beat.*] I'm gay.
   A long silence as RON, DAWN *and* KAREN *stare at him.*
RON: [*incredulous*] He's a poofter.
DEBBIE: Dad. That's offensive.
RON: You're telling me!
   DEBBIE *throws her hands in the air in frustration.*
DAWN: But you're married. To a girl. With blonde hair and eyeshadow…
MICHAEL: I know this is a huge thing to dump on you all. I don't expect you to assimilate it straight— [away.]
KAREN: [*interrupting, wrinkling her nose*] Oh, my God, this is so gross. You actually… *do things* with *other men?!*
MICHAEL: I'm intimate with one man, Karen.
RON: For Christ's sake, spare us the details!
DAWN: But I don't understand… How can you just suddenly become a… [*pausing, the word is difficult to say*] … homosexual?
MICHAEL: There's nothing sudden about it, Mum. I've known I was gay since I was sixteen.
RON: I should never have sent you on that Sea Scouts Bivouac!
DEBBIE: That's an intelligent reaction, Dad.
KAREN: How come you're so calm? He told you, didn't he? Why didn't you tell me?
MICHAEL: Mum, I'm sorry. I know this is a horrible shock…
DAWN: It's our fault. It must be our fault. Was there too much André Rieu in the house?
MICHAEL: It's not your fault, Mum. It's just a fact. And it's got nothing to do with you or Dad.
RON: You're bloody right it doesn't.
DEBBIE: Dad, will you try dragging yourself into the twenty-first century? Some of the most successful people in the world have been gay— presidents, prime ministers, football players—
RON: [*cutting across her*] Footy players? Don't talk bloody rubbish!
   MICHAEL *makes a move towards his father.*
MICHAEL: I knew this would horrify you. That's why I've never told you before. Well, I tried to tell you in my Private Moments, but as usual you wouldn't shut up for long enough to—Anyway, that's… the thing

is... I know that even if you live to be, well... [*looking at the clock*] fifty minutes older, you'll probably still never understand. But can't you at least respect me for my honesty...? Mates...? Please?

A vulnerable MICHAEL *holds out his hand to shake his father's.* RON *looks at* MICHAEL*'s hand and deliberately turns away, picking up a champagne glass instead.*

RON: I need some more champagne—

MICHAEL *sees red and lunges at him.*

MICHAEL: You arsehole!

DEBBIE, DAWN *and* KAREN *race forward to stop him.*

DAWN/DEBBIE/KAREN: Michael! / Stop! / Don't! [*etc.*]

MICHAEL: I've been living a lie for you! I did everything your damn way!

DAWN: [*overlapping, a sudden realisation*] Oh, no! The baby!

DEBBIE: What?

DAWN: [*to* MICHAEL] What's going to happen to your poor little baby?!

MICHAEL: It's alright, Mum. Monique's not pregnant.

DAWN: She's not?

MICHAEL: She's not.

RON: Then why did you tell me she was?

MICHAEL: I *didn't!*

DAWN: There's no baby...?

MICHAEL: That's right. There's no baby.

KAREN: There's no baby?

MICHAEL: Yes! There's *no* baby!

DEBBIE: Actually—there *is* a baby.

MICHAEL: Debbie, you of all people should know—we're not—

RON: [*interrupting*] Michael was just having a joke with us, Debbie. You 'gays' have got a strange sense of humour.

DAWN: So I'm not going to be a grandma.

DEBBIE: Yes, Mum. You *are*— [going to be a grandma.]

MICHAEL: [*interrupting impatiently*] How many times do I have to say this? Monique and me are *not* having a baby!

DEBBIE: *I'm* having a baby. [*Beat.*] I am. [*Beat.*] *I'm* pregnant.

DAWN/RON/MICHAEL/KAREN: What?! / You're pregnant?! [*etc.*]

DEBBIE: I wasn't going to tell anyone yet... I'm eleven weeks.

DAWN/KAREN: [*in unison*] You're... pregnant?

DEBBIE *nods.*

RON: So you *have* got a fella?

DEBBIE: For God's sake, Dad.

Beat. They all stare at her.

Look. I wasn't planning for this to happen, but it did, and now that I'm used to the idea… I'm pretty excited about it.

MICHAEL: Was it Brendan?

DEBBIE *nods.*

KAREN: Who's Brendan?

DEBBIE *remains silent.*

Nobody tells me anything.

DEBBIE: There's nothing to tell. It's over.

RON: Don't be stupid. You'll have to marry the bloke.

DEBBIE: Dad, marriage isn't obligatory anymore—I thought we'd just established that. And besides, I can't marry him. I don't love him.

DAWN: But, Debbie, you're having his baby!

DEBBIE: Mum, things have changed. A child doesn't have to be raised by two parents in the same house. Brendan will definitely be involved, but *I'll* be the primary caregiver.

RON: The primary what? Don't talk rubbish. You're getting married.

DEBBIE: I'm not getting married.

RON: Yes, you bloody are!

DEBBIE: No, I'm bloody not!

MICHAEL: Great. You want her to do the same thing I did: waste years of her life and somebody else's being totally miserable! [*Beat.*] Let me tell you something, Dad: Marriage sucks!

DAWN: Karen. Don't listen to your brother and sister. Marriage is a beautiful institution.

RON: Michael's marriage is a unique and—morally questionable situation. And Debbie's being extremely selfish. Marriage is a wonderful thing. Look at me and your mother—

KAREN: Oh, don't give me that!

They all look at her in surprise.

Everything has to go *your* way, Dad. Every little thing. And Mum tiptoes around you like a frightened mouse. [*Beat.*] If Ben and I thought *that* was marriage, we'd never do it in a million years!

DAWN *and* RON *are astounded by* KAREN*'s words. She takes a few deep breaths, regains her composure.*

I don't like being rude to my elders, but that had to be said. Maybe we should move on to the next item?

END OF ACT ONE

ACT TWO

The stage is in darkness.

The tick-tick of the clock is now joined by a knock-knock to the same beat. We may or may not realise they are separate sounds. The slide projector is turned on. Onto the now blank light on the wall a slide is projected. It's hastily and untidily scrawled. It reads: 'Late Unscheduled Item: Very Private Moments—Ron'.

The lights come up to reveal RON *standing on a chair in the middle of the living room. He has made a noose and is trying to tie it to a light fitting above his head. The noose is not around his neck as yet.*

The knock-knocking coming from the kitchen, increases in tempo and urgency.

KAREN: [*through the door*] Dad, let us in!

DEBBIE: [*through the door*] We didn't mean it!

MICHAEL: [*through the door*] You're a wonderful father!

RON: I'm a lousy father. You said so.

DEBBIE: [*through the door*] We never used that exact terminology.

KAREN: [*through the door*] I didn't mean what I said about you and Mum!

DEBBIE: [*through the door*] I didn't mean what I said about things being your fault!

MICHAEL: [*through the door*] I was joking, Dad!

    RON *stops for a moment.*

RON: You were joking?

MICHAEL: [*through the door*] Yeah.

RON: About *everything?*

MICHAEL: [*through the door*] Well. Almost. Except the homosexual bit.

    RON *goes back to securing the noose.*

RON: I want you kids to leave me alone now.

KAREN: [*hissing at* MICHAEL *through the door*] Tell him you're not gay!

MICHAEL: [*hissing back*] I can't.

KAREN: [*hissing*] It's only for another thirty-nine minutes.

MICHAEL: [*hissing*] I'm not going to!

KAREN: [*hissing*] If Debbie asked, you would!
DEBBIE: [*hissing*] For God's sake, Karen. This is hardly the time.

Unseen by RON, DAWN *enters from the other side of the room carrying two cups of steaming black coffee.* DAWN *has sobered up considerably. She's behind* RON. *She reacts at seeing him tying the noose, then composes herself.*

[*Calling through the door*] Dad. What are you doing in there?
RON: I told you. I've scheduled some private moments for myself.
KAREN: [*through the door*] Are you alright?
RON: Physically, I'm well-equipped to live until ten twenty-three. Emotionally, it's another story. [*Sighing*] But that's something I hold myself entirely responsible for. And I want you kids to know that if by some chance I don't make it to the appointed hour… [*He grunts as he fastens a difficult knot.*] Euggh.

MICHAEL, DEBBIE *and* KAREN *are frantic at these ominous words.*

KAREN: [*hissing*] He's killing himself!
DEBBIE: [*overlapping*] We've got to do something!
DEBBIE/KAREN: Michael! Do something!

MICHAEL *knocks loudly on the door.*

MICHAEL: [*through the door*] If you don't let us in we'll knock the door down!
RON: Just leave me in peace.
KAREN: [*through the door*] But what are you doing?!
DAWN: Your father's got himself all in knots. And you lot yelling through the door isn't helping.

RON *turns to look at* DAWN.

MICHAEL: [*hissing, relieved*] Mum's in there.
DEBBIE: [*overlapping*] Thank God!
KAREN: [*through the door*] Mum, we think Dad's going to—
DAWN: [*interrupting, calling*] That's enough, Karen. I want you all to respect your father's wishes for a few Private Moments.
KAREN: [*through the door*] Sorry, Mum.
DEBBIE: [*through the door*] Sorry, Dad.
MICHAEL: [*through the door*] Sorry.
DAWN: There'll be plenty of time for sorries later.

The tick-tick of the clock reminds everyone that time may be the last thing they have.

Just leave Dad alone for a bit.
MICHAEL/DEBBIE/KAREN: Okay. / Yeah. / Of course. / Sorry. [*etc.*]

Then silence from the kitchen.
RON: How did you get in here?
DAWN: I've got a spare key to the front door, as if you didn't know.

RON *ignores the implications of* DAWN*'s words. They both stare up at the noose.*

RON: Oh, I'm sorry. I know this is a cowardly act. I was going to leave you a farewell note… but you can never find a biro in this bloody place.

DAWN *pushes a cup of black coffee towards* RON.

DAWN: Have one of these, Ron. I've had four. It's sobered me up well and truly.

RON *waves the coffee away, dramatically disgusted.*

RON: I'm not *drunk*, Dawn. I'm a failure as a father. And a cup of coffee's going to do bugger-all to fix that. [*Beat.*] No, there's only one way. I have to end it.

They both look up at the noose.
DAWN: Well, that knot won't do the trick.

She pushes him off his chair.

Here. Let me try. I think I remember from Girl Guides.

She climbs up onto the chair and starts adjusting the knot.
RON: Dawn…?
DAWN: What you need is a reef knot.

RON *watches her in silent amazement, then…*

RON: And you reckon you're sober?
DAWN: You've only got half an hour left anyway. It's six of one, half a dozen of the other.
RON: I have to do it.
DAWN: I couldn't agree more.
RON: I can't live with my failure.

DAWN: And why should you, Ron? You've had thirty-eight years to be a half-hearted father. You've got thirty-eight minutes to try and make up for it. And that might mean saying sorry. And listening. You're right. It's too hard. Go ahead. Kill yourself.
RON: I *wanted* to get to know them better. I wanted to know what they were thinking and feeling. I wanted—
DAWN: [*interrupting*] You wanted them to pat you on the back and lie about how wonderful you are. But they didn't. And now you're sulking.

> DAWN *looks at* RON *challengingly. Silence. She's not going to make this easy for him.*

RON: Dawn. Our son is a *homosexual*.
DAWN: [*finding this difficult*] Yes, he is.
RON: That *must* mean I've stuffed up.
DAWN: Maybe it does.
RON: And do you think it's my fault that Debbie's got a baby on the way but no bloke to go with it?
DAWN: *She* seems to think so.
RON: Have I really been... *emotionally unavailable?*
DAWN: So she says.

> RON *looks at* DAWN *in surprise.*

RON: You're not even trying to cheer me up.
DAWN: I'm tired of cheering you up, Ron. You've got such a small amount of time left and you're trying to waste it on this pointless conversation because you're too scared to face your children.

> RON *reacts to* DAWN'*s stern tone with pride.*

RON: [*teasing*] And Karen thinks *you're* frightened of *me*.

> DAWN *simply smiles.* RON *holds out his hand and helps* DAWN *off the chair in an old-fashioned, chivalrous gesture.*

Have I really been such a lousy husband?
DAWN: Now you want *me* to tell lies about how wonderful you are.
RON: Come on... couldn't you tell me *one?*

> RON *and* DAWN *share a tender smile.*

DAWN: It's funny. They think it stops, don't they? Kids. They think you stop feeling all of those things.

RON: I'm going to miss you, Dawnie.
DAWN: I'll miss you too.

They move into a gentle kiss, then a warm and lingering hug. As they break apart...

RON: I'll let 'em in, eh…?

RON moves over to the kitchen door. He opens it and… MICHAEL, DEBBIE *and* KAREN *fall through into the living room. They've been straining at the door, trying to eavesdrop.*

MICHAEL/DEBBIE/KAREN: Oooh! / Aaggh! / We were just—
RON: You can come in now.

The kids cluster around RON. DAWN *watches on.*

KAREN: Dad. Thank God you're… [okay.]

She stops as she notices something. DEBBIE *and* MICHAEL *follow her gaze to the noose, still hanging from the ceiling. A very awkward silence, then all at once...*

I'm sorry I said that stuff about marriage. Everybody's different and just because I don't want me and Ben to be like you and Mum doesn't give me— [the right…]

DEBBIE: And I'm sorry I blamed you for me being single. I'm an adult and I have to take responsibility for my own life and if I've got some kind of issue, it's up to me to— [work it out.]

MICHAEL: And I shouldn't have tried to hit you but I was confused and when you wouldn't shake my hand I felt so hurt that— [I lashed out.]

DEBBIE, MICHAEL and KAREN have all been speaking at the same time.

RON holds up his arms to silence them.

RON: [*with a loud whistle*] Hey. Hey. Woah.

They stop. Silence for a beat.

KAREN: I'm sorrier than them, Dad. I'm the sorriest!
RON: If anyone should be making amends around here, it's *me*. [*Beat.*] Saying sor… Admitting that I've been in the wrong doesn't come easy to me. A man doesn't like to acknowledge that he could have handled things better. But that's obviously, *very obviously*, the case in my case… so…

KAREN/MICHAEL/DEBBIE: It's okay, Dad. / Don't… you know. / You don't have to say sorry… [*etc.*]
RON: [*interrupting*] No. Hear me out. [*Pause.*] I want to say that I regret my— I'm *sorry* for all my inadequacies as a father. And I love you and respect you all very much—regardless of your marital status, pregnancy situation or sexual preference.
MICHAEL/DEBBIE/KAREN: Oh, Dad… / Dad… / Oh…
DAWN: Oh, Ron, Darling…
RON: [*holding out his arms*] How about a hug?

> *They all move hesitantly and awkwardly into a communal hug.*
>
> DEBBIE *is about to hug* RON *when* KAREN *practically pushes her out of the way to get closest to him.* DAWN *joins in.* MICHAEL *is last to join the hug. He walks towards the group with his arms outstretched tentatively.*

[*Reaching for him*] Son.

> MICHAEL *joins in and the family is one hybrid embracing beast.*
>
> *A knock at the front door.*
>
> *They all remain rooted together, not wanting to break the moment. A beat or two.*
>
> *Another knock at the front door.*

ALL: [*in unison*] I'll get it.

> *Shared laughter.*

RON: I tell you what. We'll *all* get it.

> *The strange hybrid embracing beast moves as one towards the front door. Then* DEBBIE*'s back goes again.*

DEBBIE: Oooh!
RON: Are you alright, Debbie?
DAWN: Is it your tummy?
DEBBIE: No. It's my back again.
DAWN: You'll have to be careful now you're having a baby…

> *As everyone else gathers around* DEBBIE, MICHAEL *walks to the front door and opens it. A good-looking young man in a dark suit stands on the threshold. He has a polite, puppy-dog eagerness and carries a briefcase. He's* TED WILKINS.

MICHAEL: Hi. Can I help you?
TED: Good evening. [*Holding out his hand*] My name's Ted Wilkins, from Wilkins and Son Funerals.

A dazed MICHAEL *shakes his hand.*

May I offer my sincere condolences. [*Looking around the room*] To the entire family.

RON *approaches and shakes* TED'*s hand.*

Note: TED *does not notice the noose.*

RON: Ted. Pleased to meet you in person.
TED: Perhaps you could take me to the deceased.
RON: *I'm* the deceased.
TED: But you're not deceased.
RON: I won't be deceased until ten twenty-three.
TED: But it's... [*looking at his watch*] eleven-o-seven.
RON: No. It's nine fifty-seven.
TED: No. It's eleven— [*He looks at the clock on the wall, realises.*] Oh. I'm terribly sorry. I've still got my watch set on Daylight Saving. [*He gives another polite smile around the room.*] Guess I'll just have to wait then.

He plonks himself down on a chair. They all stare at him.

Please don't let me intrude. Just go on with whatever you were doing.

Another nonplussed silence. Then DAWN *picks up a plate from the table and proffers it to* TED.

DAWN: Can I offer you a Salada?
TED: [*taking one with a polite smile*] Thank you.
RON: Ted. This is Dawn Patterson. The best wife a man ever had.
DAWN: Oh, Ron...
TED: I'm delighted to meet you, Mrs Patterson.
DAWN: And these are our three kids. We've had our differences in the past—and some people were more aware of that than others—but I'm pleased to say we've patched things up in plenty of time for the funeral.

TED *smiles with polite interest.*

RON: This is Karen. The baby of the family. She's getting married soon.
TED: Oh. Please accept my congratulations along with my condolences.
KAREN: Thank you.

RON: But she's doing it *her* way, Ted. She's learning from me and her mother's mistakes, and *she's* going to be the boss!
KAREN: I didn't mean that, Dad. I got carried away. It was Michael and Debbie's fault. They made me—
RON: Sssh. Hey. I respect you for having an opinion, Princess. And this is our eldest daughter. Debbie.

He squeezes DEBBIE. *It hurts her back. She winces.*

DEBBIE: Hi.
TED: Nice to meet you.
RON: Debbie's single.
TED: [*polite*] Oh?
RON: And she's having a baby.
DEBBIE: Dad!
RON: [*jovially*] She slept with a bloke but she didn't love him.

TED nods politely.

A lot of girls do that these days. Debbie's got a wonderful job and lots of close friends. And hobbies and so on. Her life's very fulfilled.

TED nods again.

Dawn and I are extremely proud of her. Especially *me*. And I'm interested in everything she does, no matter how small or insignificant.
TED: Well. It must be nice to have such an attentive father.

RON squeezes DEBBIE *again. She winces in pain.*

RON: And that handsome bloke over there is my son Michael.
TED: We met at the door. Hello again.

RON puts his arm around MICHAEL *and* MICHAEL *realises with horror what he is about to say as…*

RON: Michael's a homosexual.

Stunned silence. Except from MICHAEL.

MICHAEL: Christ.
RON: But it makes no difference to me and Dawn. We still love him just as much as we ever have.

TED nods politely.

And he loves a bloke called Alex! Don't you, Mate?
MICHAEL: Andrew.

RON: Yeah. Of course. Absolutely. Shame I'll never get to meet the man who makes my son so happy. [*He's trying so hard to be cool about this, but finding it very difficult.*] Tell us a bit about him, Michael. How did you two fellas get together?

> MICHAEL *looks towards* DAWN. *This is hardly an appropriate time or place.*

MICHAEL: Dad…

RON: [*following his gaze*] No. Come on. Your mother's just as interested as I am.

DAWN: [*with a supportive smile*] Of course I am, Sweetheart.

RON: We're all interested. Aren't we? [*Beat.*] Girls?

DEBBIE: Absolutely.

KAREN: You may as well tell us.

> MICHAEL *looks hesitantly towards* TED.

TED: Please. Don't mind me.

MICHAEL: Well, he's been a colleague for a few years. But we were working late one night a few months ago and… [*Smiling at the memory*] He kissed me. That was the night we became lovers.

> *At the word 'lovers'* RON *nearly has a fit. He tries to hide it with a huge phoney smile.*

RON: R-i-i-i-g-h-t! How about another cuppa? Dawn, I'll give you a hand.

> RON *exits into the kitchen as fast as his legs will carry him, dragging* DAWN *behind.*

DAWN: Excuse us for a moment, Ted.

> RON *and* DAWN *exit.* TED *smiles at the kids, genuinely moved.*

TED: I must say it's very refreshing to meet such an open and communicative family.

KAREN: Oh, Dad's always been pretty relaxed about that sort of stuff.

> *From the kitchen we hear…*

DAWN: [*off*] Ron, calm down! You're hyperventilating!

> KAREN *looks at* MICHAEL *in annoyance, forgetting* TED *for a moment.*

KAREN: You shouldn't have told him.

MICHAEL: He had to find out sometime.

KAREN: But he didn't have to find out *tonight!*
MICHAEL: We all have to hear things we don't want to hear, Karen.
KAREN: You're just selfish.
DEBBIE: Karen—
KAREN: [*interrupting*] And so are you, Debbie. You two think you're so smart with all your little secrets.
DEBBIE: Oh, here we go.
MICHAEL: Why are you so paranoid?
KAREN: I'm not paranoid. You never tell me anything. But you tell each other *everything.*
MICHAEL: Debbie didn't tell me she was having a baby.
KAREN: Huh. Debbie shouldn't be having a baby.

  DEBBIE *looks at* KAREN *in disbelief.*

You've got no respect for the father, whoever he is, and you'll have no support with the poor little child—
DEBBIE: I told you Brendan will be involved—
KAREN: [*yelling*] And you're going to be fat at my wedding! [*A few beats as she calms herself down.*] You're going to be an unmarried mother, Debbie. How do you think that makes Dad feel?
DEBBIE: How about how *I* feel?
KAREN: How *you* feel doesn't matter. Dad just might be dying tonight!
MICHAEL: He's not going to die.
TED: But he rang and booked.

  They all look at TED, *suddenly remembering his presence.*

MICHAEL: I'm afraid we're probably wasting your time, Ted.
DEBBIE: But if we are, Michael and I will compensate you for—
KAREN: *I'll* give him some money too.
DEBBIE: But, Karen. You're always saying you have to save for the wedding.
KAREN: Why do you always have to bring up my wedding? They just want to spoil it for me, Ted.
DEBBIE: [*turning to* TED] What did I say? Did I sound like I wanted to spoil it to you?
TED: [*trying to stay neutral*] Well, I—
MICHAEL: [*interrupting*] You've got problems, Karen. [*To* TED] Wouldn't you say so?

KAREN *taps* TED *on the shoulder to get his attention.*

KAREN: They hate me because they think I'm Dad's favourite.

DEBBIE: You *are* Dad's favourite.

MICHAEL: She's definitely his favourite.

TED: Your father doesn't seem to have a favourite to me. He's very loving with all of you.

KAREN: See? See?

MICHAEL: Ted. Let me set you straight on a few things here. I bet you thought Dad's known I'm gay for years? That he's been comfortable with it since the 1990s. Right?

TED: Well, yes, I did think that…

MICHAEL: And I don't blame you, Ted. Because the man you've met tonight bears *no resemblance* to the father we've had for thirty-eight years.

TED: That seems a little harsh to me—

DEBBIE: It's not, Ted. Michael's telling the truth. You haven't seen what Dad's really like.

TED: I've seen enough to know that he's open-hearted and deeply loving.

RON *re-enters. He's sewn his smile back on.*

RON: Well. Dawn seems to have the tea under control. [*With a smile to* MICHAEL] Lovers, eh? That's, ah… Yeah, terrific.

MICHAEL *squirms under* RON*'s ultra-'relaxed' smile.*

The tick-tick of the clock.

TED: Mr Patterson. I wonder if you'd be interested in taking this opportunity to participate in a few decisions about your funeral? I usually discuss these matters with close relatives post-death, but seeing we've got about [*looking to the clock*] twenty-five minutes prior to the cessation of life, I thought you might like to be involved.

RON: Why not?

Beaming excitedly from ear to ear, TED *moves to his briefcase and opens it.*

TED: I've never dealt directly with the deceased before, so I hope you'll bear with me while I feel my way.

RON *glances at the clock as* TED *rummages in his briefcase.*

RON: Take your time, Ted. No pressure.

TED: Now, Mr Patterson…

> DAWN *re-enters with a tray full of teacups.*

The first thing I have to do is measure you for your coffin.

DAWN: He's five feet ten inches. Has been since the day I first met him at the ice-skating rink in 1967. My lace was undone. Ron offered to tie it. [*Smiling*] Five feet ten, Ted.

> DAWN *hands out teacups. Ad lib thank-you's, etc.*

TED: I don't mean to doubt your word, Mrs Patterson, but sometimes as people get older and life's worries take their toll, they can start to lose an inch or two…

RON: After all the things I've found out tonight I'm probably four foot eleven, then!

> *They all laugh a tad uncomfortably.* RON *nudges* MICHAEL.

Just a joke, Son. I'm completely comfortable with your lifestyle. And very supportive.

MICHAEL: Thanks, Dad.

TED: I seem to have left my tape measure back at the morgue. Would you have some string, or… *rope* perhaps…?

> *As* TED *is speaking he moves to a point where he is standing directly under the noose. An embarrassed reaction from the Pattersons as they look up at it.*

RON: Well, what do you know? We do have some… ah, rope.

> TED *follows* RON*'s gaze and gulps down his tea in shock at the sight of the noose.* RON *starts to carry a chair over to the noose.* KAREN *takes it from him.*

KAREN: Here, Dad. I'll do that.

RON: Thanks, Sweetie.

> *They all watch uncomfortably as* KAREN *climbs onto the chair and unties the noose. Another silence.*

DAWN: Ted? How's your tea?

TED: [*shell-shocked*] Delicious thank you, Mrs Patterson.

> DEBBIE *shoves a plate of cold party pies in front of him.*

DEBBIE: Party pie?

TED: Ah, I hope you won't think that I'm being presumptuous, but I'd just like to say that I really think you're quite a remarkable family unit.
DAWN: Thank you, Ted.
TED: If all families could be as open as yours, funerals would be a lot more fun to attend. [*Beat.*] Ah, not that they're supposed to be fun, of course.

> KAREN *is off the chair. She hands* TED *the rope.*

KAREN: Here, Ted.
TED: Thank you. [*He turns to* RON.] What I'll do is get you to stand up straight, Mr Patterson, and if someone could hold the bottom of the rope while I measure it up to your height and mark it.

> TED *reaches into his suit pocket and gets out a pen as* MICHAEL *takes the bottom of the rope.*

MICHAEL: Here… I'll do it.

> MICHAEL *holds the rope near the bottom of* RON*'s foot.*

RON: You right there, Son? [*Jovially*] Keep away from that inside leg!

> MICHAEL *grimaces in irritation.*

Just a little joke.
MICHAEL: Right, Dad… [*His BlackBerry starts ringing.*] Excuse me. Here, Deb.

> DEBBIE *takes* MICHAEL*'s end of the rope while* MICHAEL *moves off to answer his BlackBerry. Meanwhile,* TED *takes the other end of the rope and holds it up against* RON.

[*Into the BlackBerry*] Yeah, Phil, did you get him? Shit! Have you called him? Emailed? Texted? Tweeted? Well, *find him*—we're going to have London, Dubai and San Francisco back on the line in ten minutes—unless you've stuffed *that* up, too?

> MICHAEL *walks off into the background, continuing the call.*

DAWN: Are you sure you should be crouching, Debbie? Maybe Karen could…
DEBBIE: [*good-natured*] I'm pregnant, Mum. I'm not an invalid.
KAREN: Yeah. She's not an invalid.
RON: What about your back? Is it giving you trouble?
DEBBIE: No. It's fine at the moment, Dad.
KAREN: *Mine's* hurting a bit.

RON: Oh, Sweetie…
DEBBIE: Since when?

> TED *is holding his end of the rope up against* RON*'s head with a biro in the other hand, but as* RON *won't keep his head still, the measuring process is proving a difficult task.* TED *is starting to feel a tad put out.*

TED: Please…
DAWN: Stand up straight, Ron. If you slump you'll be shorter than five foot ten and you don't want to feel cramped in your coffin.
TED: [*marking the rope with biro*] Right. Got that. Thanks, Mr Patterson.

> TED *takes the rope and starts rolling it.* DEBBIE *rolls from the other end. They meet in the middle.* RON *looks on.*

RON: You know, you two look great together. Don't they, Dawn?
DEBBIE: Dad…
RON: Are you married, Ted?
TED: [*putting the rope in his briefcase*] No, I'm not.

> RON *raises his eyebrows significantly at* DEBBIE.

RON: Like babies, do you?
DAWN: Ron. Ssssh…

> TED *picks up a folder from his briefcase.*

TED: Now you might like to choose a coffin. I have photographs of the different styles and finishes we offer. If you'd all like to gather around…
DAWN: Michael. Come and help us, Sweetheart.

> *As* MICHAEL *wanders over and stands behind the couch:*

MICHAEL: [*into his BlackBerry*] Try his wife again. I *don't care* if you woke her up—we're going to have egg all over our faces! Yeah, I'll hold.

> MICHAEL *looks over his family's heads at the coffin photos while he waits for Phil to get back to him. Meanwhile,* RON *pushes* DEBBIE *towards* TED.

RON: Debbie. You're chief advisor. [*To* TED] Debbie knows a lot about styles and finishes. She's an interior designer.
TED: Oh?
RON: A talented one too. We're all very proud.

> TED *registers this with a polite smile.*

KAREN: Are you prouder of Debbie than you are of me?
DAWN: Dad's proud of you all exactly the same. Aren't you, Ron?
RON: Spot-on, Dawn. Isn't that so, Ted?
TED: It certainly seems that way to me. [*He turns his attention back to the folder.*] We start off with the basic model, which is comprised of particle board with unlaquered finish. And the handles and personally engraved plaque are gold-plated.
   The family gazes at the photograph in the folder.
KAREN: It looks cheap.
MICHAEL: No style.
DAWN: Not shiny enough.
RON: [*to* TED] Debbie's a good cook too—and you should see her flat—always spick and span…
   DEBBIE *nudges her mother sharply:* Help me!
DAWN: Now, Ron. Pay attention to the coffins. *You're* the one who has to live in the thing.
   She laughs at her unconscious pun. Everyone joins in.
   Live in it! Ooh, that's funny. Anyway. Pay attention.
   RON *throws his arm around* DAWN *and turns to* KAREN.
RON: And you think *I* give the orders!
KAREN: [*guiltily*] Dad…
DAWN: It's alright, Sweetheart. We know you didn't mean any malice.
RON: You were concerned. And no wonder. You're about to take that big step yourself. Did I tell you Karen's getting married, Ted?
TED: Yes, you did. Congratulations again.
RON: If you're thinking she looks younger than Debbie, you're right. There's ten years between them. Debbie's thirty-six.
TED: Really?
RON: But as far as we're concerned she's still a spring chicken. And we're proud of the fact that she's single.
   TED *nods with a smile.*
   And pregnant.
   DEBBIE *is incredibly mortified.*
   Have you got a girlfriend, Ted?
DEBBIE: [*mortified*] Can we move onto the next coffin?

TED: [*referring back to his folder*] Of course. This is our newest line—the eco-coffin. It's made of naturally occurring materials that dissolve into the earth and enrich it with nutrients.

DEBBIE: [*enthusiastically*] That looks *great*—

RON: [*cutting across her*] No bloody way! I'm not lying in a coffin that turns to compost!

> DAWN *nudges* RON. DEBBIE *looks a little hurt.* RON *quickly backtracks.*

[*To* DEBBIE, *conciliatory*] I mean, not unless *you* think I should, Sweetie?

DEBBIE: Not if *you* don't, Dad.

> RON *looks extremely relieved.* TED *turns back to his folder.*

TED: Well… we also have the cedar coffin with natural polish.

> *Everyone murmers in approval.*

It's a middle-of-the-road model that's a popular choice for the deceased we deal with. Those handles come in silver or gold.

DEBBIE: That's nice.

DAWN: It looks dignified.

MICHAEL: I don't mind that.

KAREN: I like it.

MICHAEL: [*into his BlackBerry, as Phil returns*] Yeah, I'm here. What took you so long?

> *He wanders off to resume his conversation.*

> *A silence as the others wait for* RON *to express his opinion on the cedar coffin.*

DAWN: Ron? What do you think?

RON: I'm leaving the decision up to Debbie. She's the decor expert in the family.

DEBBIE: You're sure you trust my decisions?

RON: Completely.

DEBBIE: Then we'll take that one. With silver handles.

RON: Gold.

DEBBIE: What?

RON: Just a suggestion.

DEBBIE: See? You *don't* trust me!

RON: I trust you! [*To* TED] Silver.
DEBBIE: No. He wants gold.
RON: No. I want silver.
DEBBIE: He's lying.
RON: I'm not lying. I want silver.
DAWN: But, Ron—you did say gold.
RON: I've changed my mind. I want silver.
DAWN: But you don't like silver.
RON: I love silver.
DAWN: No, you don't.
RON: *I'm* the corpse. *I* know what I want on my coffin!
MICHAEL: [*trying to hear on his BlackBerry*] Ssssh!
DEBBIE: I can't do anything right by you, can I? Nothing I do is right!
DAWN: Now, Debbie…
DEBBIE: You said you're sorry and you want to take an interest, but you still can't trust me, can you?!
DAWN: Think of the baby, Darling.
DEBBIE: You keep saying you're proud but you don't mean it. You won't even let me pick your coffin handles!
MICHAEL: Ssssh!
RON: I'm letting you pick them! *Silver*, for Christ's sake!
DEBBIE: And you say you couldn't care less that I'm single, but all you've been doing for the last fifteen minutes is trying to set me up with an *undertaker!* [*Turning to* TED] No offence, Ted.
TED: [*crestfallen*] None taken.
DEBBIE: You either ignore me or pick-pick-pick. It has to be one or the other. You think I'm stupid, don't you? You—
RON: No, Debbie. *I'm* the stupid one.
DEBBIE: You got *that* right.
KAREN: Debbie! Mum—did you hear that?!

> MICHAEL *gives* KAREN *a disparaging look as* RON *moves over and puts his arm around* DEBBIE.

RON: Your sister's spot-on, Karen. Sometimes your old dad's a few kangaroos short in the top paddock.
DEBBIE: Oh, I didn't mean it…
RON: [*sincerely*] No. You're absolutely right. I was being a dill. Gold's too flashy for a dead bloke.

DEBBIE *recognises the backdown for the apology and concession it is. She smiles as* RON *kisses the top of her head. A reconciliation. A real one.* RON *squeezes her tight.* KAREN *watches, miffed.*

MICHAEL: [*into the BlackBerry*] Well, find him, Phil, or you'll be finding your way to the dole queue!

MICHAEL hangs up.

The tick-tick of the clock.

They all look to the wall.

KAREN: Fifteen minutes.

She virtually pulls DEBBIE *and* RON *apart.*

Oh, Dad, I can't believe you'll be gone so soon.

RON: Fifteen minutes and it'll all be over.

DAWN: Don't say that, Ron. It'll just be beginning.

Beat. RON *looks unconvinced.*

It *will*. You'll be going on a new and wonderful journey…

RON: Yeah. All the way from here to the cemetery. And instead of a bus I'll be catching a coffin, eh, Ted?

DAWN: No, Ron—you'll float down a long white tunnel—and Grandad will be at the end, waiting for you with his arms wide open!

KAREN: Oh, Mum, do you think so…?

DAWN: [*nodding*] Of course I do. And Grandma Hurley will be there too—

KAREN: Oh, and Blacky! Do you think Dad will see Blacky again?

DAWN: Of course he will.

MICHAEL *and* DEBBIE *also have very fond memories of Blacky.*

MICHAEL/DEBBIE: Oh, good old Blacky. / I'd love to see Blacky…

RON: Who the hell is Blacky?

DAWN: That labrador we had for eleven years, Ron.

RON: Oh, yeah. Right. Of course.

DAWN: Will you give Grandma Hurley a great big hug for me and tell her I found her brooch behind the kitchen cabinet?

RON: I will if I see her.

DAWN: Of course you'll see her.

RON: I'm not making any promises, Dawn. It depends on life after death.

DAWN: I wish you'd have more faith, Ron. There *is* life after death. There *is*.

RON: [*trying to joke*] I'll let you know.
KAREN: Oh, could you, Dad? [*Beat.*] We could think of a signal. So we know your spirit's here with us.
Shocked reactions around the room.
MICHAEL: Karen. That is the most ridiculous idea—
RON: I like the idea. Ted, would you have an ethical problem with that?
TED: Not at all!
RON: Well. I tell you what. I'll knock like this… [*Demonstrating a distinct knocking pattern*] And then I'll smash [*pointing*] The Bounty.
DAWN: Oh, Ron, not *The Bounty*.
RON: Alright. I won't smash anything. But I'll knock like this… [*Demonstrating the knocking pattern again*] If you hear that you'll know I'm in the room. Got it?
They all nod with varying degrees of discomfort. DAWN *doesn't like talking about this stuff.*
DAWN: Ah, Ted, perhaps we should get back to the funeral arrangements?
TED: Well, maybe we could move onto the topic of hymns for the service. Strictly speaking this is between the family and the minister, but considering that I'm here and so are you, Mr Patterson…
RON: I want them to sing my favourite song.
KAREN: Dad, you can't sing 'What's New Pussycat?' at a funeral.
RON: Tom Jones. You know it?
TED: [*getting a hymn book from his briefcase*] It's probably more appropriate to choose a hymn from the traditional selections—
RON: I don't give a rat's ring what's appropriate, Ted.
DAWN: Ron!
RON: Is it appropriate for Karen to tell me and Dawn how we should conduct our marriage?
KAREN: Dad—
RON: Is it appropriate for Debbie to be carrying the kid of some bloke she's hardly clapped eyes on—?
DEBBIE: Dad—
RON: Is it appropriate for Michael to be kissing some fella behind the photocopier—?
DAWN: Ron, please. You're being ill-mannered.
TED: [*ever polite*] It's alright, Mrs Patterson. I take your husband's point. I'm sure it can be arranged.

RON: And I want Michael to sing it.
MICHAEL: What?
RON: Solo.
MICHAEL: You're kidding.
RON: You're my only son. That's the way I want it.
MICHAEL: You've got to be off your rocker.
RON: Just gird your loins and go for it, Son.
MICHAEL: I'm not going to sing 'What's New Pussycat?' at your funeral.
RON: Of course you are.
MICHAEL: No, I'm not.

> RON *starts wheezing for effect.*

DAWN: Michael. If it's what your father wants…
KAREN: [*overlapping*] It wouldn't kill you to do this one little thing.
DEBBIE: [*overlapping*] It'll be over in a minute. It won't be that bad—
MICHAEL: But I've got the worst singing voice in the world!
RON: Rubbish. All you homosexual fellas can sing. And dance. And write poetry.
MICHAEL: That's the most ignorant— [generalisation, etc.]
DEBBIE: Maybe we should move along. Ted. What else do we need to decide?
TED: I'd like to have a general idea about numbers. Now I'm assuming that the first two pews will be taken up with relatives. Is that a safe assumption?
RON: That depends on whether Lorraine and Barry are there.
DAWN: She's your sister, Ron. Of course she'll be there.
RON: But they're up in Surfers. [*To* TED, *by way of explanation*] I was going to warn her about the funeral but she's got her heart set on seeing the polar bears at Sea World.

> TED *nods understandingly.*

DAWN: We'll make up at least the first pew anyway. Debbie and me, and Karen and Ben, and Michael and Monique—
RON: And Angus.
MICHAEL: It's Andrew.
RON: Yeah.
MICHAEL: [*overlapping*] But he won't be there.
RON: Why not?

MICHAEL: Oh, come on.
RON: He's the man you love, isn't he? Surely he could come along to offer you some emotional support…? [*He tries not to wince.*] You'll need a hand to hold… a comforting… cuddle.
MICHAEL: Dad. Monique will be there.
RON: You said Monique knows about him.
MICHAEL: She does. But that doesn't make it appropriate.
RON: Have you had earmuffs on, Mate? I don't care what's appropriate anymore.
MICHAEL: [*sighing heavily*] Dad. It's not a good idea for me to bring Monique *and* Andrew to your funeral.
RON: But she knows about him.
MICHAEL: That doesn't mean she likes it!
RON: She may not like it but she'll have to get used to it.
MICHAEL: It's not that simple.
RON: Yes, it is. Your mother and me have managed.
MICHAEL: Monique's in a lot of pain, Dad.
RON: We all feel for her, Son. But she'll just have to take a leaf out of my book and come to terms with the situation.
MICHAEL: Oh, don't give me that bullshit!
DAWN: Michael!
MICHAEL: The only thing you've ever come to terms with is the sound of your own voice!

Shocked reactions from the family.

I wish I'd never told you I was gay! At least when we were lying we were being honest!
RON: Now, Mate. Don't you start that kind of—
MICHAEL: [*interrupting*] You don't understand it. You don't respect it. So for Christ's sake stop pretending that you do!
KAREN: Dad's just being supportive, Michael.
MICHAEL: Bullshit, Karen. He's fucking performing!
DAWN: Don't use that language in this house!
MICHAEL: I'm sorry, Mum, but that's how I feel.
DAWN: Your father's doing his best…
KAREN: It isn't easy for men Dad's age…
DEBBIE: I know he's hopeless, but he *is* genuinely trying…
TED: Your father's making a very real effort, Michael.

A short silence.

MICHAEL: If he's really making such an effort—*Ted*—why hasn't he taken me aside? Why hasn't he asked me anything about it? [*Looking to the clock, then turning to* RON] You think you're going to be dead in eleven minutes, and you haven't spent two seconds alone with me since you found out. You haven't bothered to *ask* me what it means.

    RON *is genuinely repentant.*

RON: I'm sorry, Son. Let's do that now, then. Let's talk about this. Together. Alone.

DAWN: That's a lovely idea. We'll leave you to it, then.

    DAWN, KAREN *and* DEBBIE *exit to the kitchen.* DAWN *turns at the doorway.*

Don't be too long, Sweethearts. Time's running out.

    RON *and* MICHAEL *are about to have a heart-to-heart when they realise that* TED *is still present, eagerly and supportively anticipating their reconciliation. He's watching them with interest. They are nonplussed.* DAWN *pops her head back in.*

Ted. Would you like to help us wash up some teacups?

    TED *shakes his head in a polite refusal. A more pointed look from* DAWN *and then he realises, getting to his feet.*

TED: What a good idea, Mrs Patterson. People will no doubt be dropping in to offer their condolences.

    TED *follows* DAWN *into the kitchen. On the way out he turns and gives* RON *a crossed-fingers, good-luck gesture.*

    DAWN *and* TED *exit.*

    RON *and* MICHAEL *stand facing each other, about to communicate for the first time ever.*

RON: Well, Son. I'm here, and I'm listening. Tell me how you feel.

    MICHAEL *struggles to find the right words.*

MICHAEL: I feel— [*His BlackBerry starts ringing.*] Damn! Excuse me. [*He checks the incoming call number before answering.*] Yeah, Phil? You've got 'em *all* on the line, even Boston? Way to go! Yeah, I want to brief them on the due diligence first—but I can't do it now.

You'll have to re-schedule the call, Mate. [*He holds the BlackBerry out as Phil yells in disbelief.*] Sorry, I'm in the middle of something important. I'll call you back.

As MICHAEL *is talking on the phone,* RON *silently gasps and flails his arms, trying unsuccessfully to catch his attention. Then he falls onto a chair, suddenly still. His eyes are open and he's sitting up, completely still.* MICHAEL *hangs up. He doesn't look at his father closely. He's too busy trying to find the words.*

Sorry about that. Dad, I'm so glad that I'm finally getting the chance to tell you how I feel. It's been… well, it's been hell, trying to be something I wasn't, and then finally admitting it to myself and *still* having to hide it. So you can imagine how… liberated I'm feeling now… but sad too… because I know this isn't the way you ever thought things would turn out. I know this is pretty hard to deal with, so just, let it sink in. Take some time. Take the rest of your life if you want, because… [*He smiles.*] God. It's so great to have you *listening* to me, giving me your full attention, not, you know, interrupting, and… [*He moves to* RON *with the intention of hugging him.*] Dad. I know I'm not the physically affectionate type, but, well… I just want you to know that— Dad? Dad, what…? You're not…? Dad? Dad?!

He takes a close look at his father. RON *is dead.* MICHAEL *can't believe it. The hug turns into a stranglehold around* RON*'s neck.*

You fucking bastard!

In his shock and fury he accidentally drops his BlackBerry to the floor and treads on it, smashing it. He barely notices. He grabs his lifeless father and starts shaking his shoulders.

[*Yelling*] You'd do *anything* not to listen to me! [*Wildly looking at the clock*] It's only ten thirteen, you arrogant arsehole!

    DAWN *enters, followed by* KAREN, DEBBIE *and* TED.

DAWN: Michael! Why are you screaming at your poor— [father?]
MICHAEL: [*interrupting*] He's dead!

    DAWN, DEBBIE, KAREN *and* TED *race over to* RON.

The bastard's dead!
KAREN: But it's only ten thirteen!

DAWN: He must be joking. [*Looking at* RON, *he laughs very feebly.*] Ha ha ha ha…
MICHAEL: He's not joking. Look at this.

He holds one of RON*'s arms up in the air, then drops it. It flops lifelessly.*

He's definitely carked it.

KAREN: [*to* RON] But you're not supposed to die for ten minutes! It's only ten thirteen!

DAWN: Debbie. What does your watch say?

DEBBIE *makes a dazed gesture. She doesn't speak.*

Karen? Sweetheart…?

KAREN: I'm not wearing one.

MICHAEL *picks up his smashed BlackBerry.*

MICHAEL: My BlackBerry's busted.

They all turn to look at TED.

TED: My watch is no good. It's still set on Daylight Saving.

MICHAEL: You just subtract an hour, stupid! Tell us—

DAWN: [*interrupting*] Michael. There's no need for rudeness.

MICHAEL: Just tell us what your watch says.

TED: Eleven twenty-four—twenty-five.

MICHAEL *lunges at him.*

MICHAEL: There's a ten-minute difference, you stupid, fucking undertaker!

KAREN: Michael! It's not Ted's— [fault.]

MICHAEL *chases* TED *around a lounge chair.*

MICHAEL: Why didn't you tell us the clock was ten minutes slow?!

TED: How do you know your clock's slow? Maybe my watch is ten minutes fast.

MICHAEL *bails* TED *up against a wall. He grabs him by the scruff of the neck.*

MICHAEL: Alright. I'm going to ring Andrew and check the time—and if this clock is ten minutes slow, you'd better head back to your undertaker's office and come back with a hearse built for two, pal!

MICHAEL *starts dialling.*

DAWN: Michael. Don't be so mean.

KAREN: It's not his fault.

    MICHAEL *tightens his grip on* TED.

MICHAEL: If Andrew tells me it's ten twenty-four, you're history.
KAREN: Michael, calm down!
DAWN: I'm terribly sorry about this, Ted.
TED: [*from his uncomfortable position held by the scruff of the neck*] It's alright, Mrs Patterson. Different people react to the sudden death of a loved one in very different ways.

    Andrew answers.

MICHAEL: [*to Andrew, on the phone*] Babe, it's me—what time does your iPhone say? [*Pause as Andrew asks why.*] Just tell me the time! [*He listens.*] Ten twenty-six p.m…!
TED: Don't hurt me!

    But MICHAEL *drops both* TED *and the phone and sinks onto the floor. He starts sobbing. Meanwhile* TED *tries to get himself back in order.*

DAWN: Oh, Sweetheart.
MICHAEL: I'm so tired of Dad always having the last word… [*Beat. His shoulders heave.*] He always has to have the last word.
DAWN: Oh, Sweetheart…

    She instinctively moves to the sobbing MICHAEL. *Meanwhile* DEBBIE *sits in stunned silence.*

There, there…

    KAREN *moves over to* RON *and props him back up.* TED *watches helplessly.*

TED: Please let me be the first to offer my sincere condolences. Post-death, I mean.
DAWN: Thank you, Ted.
TED: Ron was a very highly regarded member of the community, as well as a loving husband and father—
MICHAEL: Don't give us the spiel. You never met him before tonight.
TED: Maybe. But it only took half an hour to see that he was a truly wonderful father.
DAWN: No, Ted. He wasn't a wonderful father. But he tried his heart out tonight, and that will have to be enough for us. [*Beat.*] Now I'd like you to leave us alone with him, please.

TED: Of course. I've got some paperwork I can do in the hearse. I'll be back in a few minutes.

> DAWN *smiles.* TED *nods respectfully and exits. Left alone, they all gaze at* RON. DEBBIE *is in a daze.*

DEBBIE: I didn't believe it…
DAWN: He's gone.
DEBBIE: I didn't think he'd really die…
DAWN: I've lost my darling…

> *She gently touches* RON*'s face.*

We've all lost our beautiful, bombastic darling.
DEBBIE: Is this…? I can't believe this is happening…

> DEBBIE *looks away, then puts her head in her hands.* DAWN *walks over and puts her arms around her.*

KAREN: He looks so pale.
MICHAEL: What do you expect?
KAREN: But he looks… unhealthy.
MICHAEL: Karen. He's *dead*.
KAREN: He wouldn't want to look like that. He thought he was handsome.
DAWN: He *was* handsome. [*Beat.*] He *is* handsome.

> KAREN *quietly reaches into her handbag and gets out her cosmetics bag. As* DAWN *comforts* DEBBIE *and* MICHAEL *stares at her listlessly, she applies rouge and lipstick to her dead father's face with infinite tenderness.*

DEBBIE: The baby will never know him…
DAWN: Oh, Sweetheart…
MICHAEL: I'm going to sue the clock company. I'm going to take them for every penny they've got.
DAWN: It was my fault, Michael. I forgot to replace the batteries.
MICHAEL: It wasn't your fault. Dad did it deliberately. I bet he tampered with the clock. Just so he could have the last word.
DAWN: Now you're being silly.

> MICHAEL *starts heading towards the clock. He rips it off the wall, a maniac with a mission. He pulls it apart.*

MICHAEL: It would be just like him. All my life he's never listened to me, he's just talked at me. This is the first time he's spent five silent minutes since 1974!

KAREN: Shut up, Michael!

MICHAEL: He died to spite me, I'm telling you…

KAREN: [*to* RON] Don't listen to him!

> DAWN *and* DEBBIE *look around and see* RON *wearing make-up.*

DAWN: [*touched*] Oh, Karen…

KAREN: How does he look?

DEBBIE: [*not harsh*] Like a corpse with lipstick.

> *Sniffles all around.*

DAWN: He looks lovely.

> *They all pause and gaze at him. Then* DAWN *has an idea.*

Let's take one last family slide. At home with the Pattersons. Michael. The camera's in the top of the cabinet.

> MICHAEL *hesitates.*

DAWN: Come on, Sweetheart. One last slide.

MICHAEL: What's the point? He's—

KAREN: The point is Mum wants to. And so do we.

> DEBBIE *nods and sniffles.*

DEBBIE: Come on, Michael.

> *Against his better judgement* MICHAEL *moves to the cabinet and gets out the camera.*

DAWN: You know how to use the self-timer, don't you?

> MICHAEL *is setting the camera up on the edge of the table and looking through the lense.*

MICHAEL: I've got to say, I find this is a bit weird.

DAWN: [*interrupting*] What's weird about taking a family slide? Sorry, Ron, what's that?

> *She leans forward to listen as though* RON *were whispering to her.*

Your father says shut up and take the photo.

> *The kids look at* DAWN *in surprise. The mood changes a little and hysteria takes over.*

DEBBIE: He didn't say that.
DAWN: He did so.
DEBBIE: He can't talk, Mum. [*Beat.*] He's dead as a dodo.

> *A moment's shocked silence. Then* KAREN *joins in the game.*

KAREN: He's kicked the bucket.
DAWN: He's pushing up daisies.

> *They giggle.* MICHAEL *is disapproving.*

MICHAEL: [*fiddling with the camera*] I don't believe this.
DEBBIE: [*overlapping, laughing*] He's like the parrot from Monty Python. He's ceased to be.
KAREN: You're a very dead daddy.

> *The women giggle again. Their inane giggles turn tearful.*

DAWN: [*sniffling and smiling*] Your father said to hurry up, Michael.
MICHAEL: What's his rush? He's not going anywhere.

> *The women erupt into giggles again.*

DAWN: [*to* RON] Listen to your cheeky son.
MICHAEL: [*leaning over, looking through the lense*] He needs to be a bit more to the left. A bit more. Yeah. That's fine. Now, Mum...

> DAWN *leans forward to listen to* MICHAEL. *The dead* RON *promptly falls behind her on the couch. Much laughter as the women prop him up again.*

... Pick him up. Yeah. That's it. Now lean in a bit... Right. Is everybody ready?

> DEBBIE *and* KAREN *nod.* DEBBIE *moves* RON's *head from side to side in a 'no' gesture. The women laugh again.*

Debbie!
DAWN: Dad's ready too.
MICHAEL: Wait. Maybe... Could you make him smile?

> DEBBIE *holds up her father's lips in a smile.*

That's good—well, it'll do.
DAWN: Look at your daddy. He's happy as Larry!
MICHAEL: Okay. Here goes—

> MICHAEL *puts the self-timer on and runs into the photograph.*

DAWN: Quickly, Michael!
KAREN: Quick! Over here!
DAWN: Everybody look at the camera!

It's a very bizarre picture of the family with the dead RON *covered in make-up in the middle. They're all laughing.*

DEBBIE: Smile if you died five minutes ago!

*This time—in spite of himself—*MICHAEL *laughs too. The flash and click of the camera. The shocked and laughing group breaks up.*

But then what?

A long silence as they all look at each other in utter futility. It's a moment of very deep sadness.

DAWN: Oh, dear. Imagine if your poor father could hear us being so disrespectful.

At the front door, the distinct knocking pattern that RON *described earlier. The family stops and stares at each other in shock. An awed silence for a beat or two, then...*

The door opens and TED *enters, carrying a sheet.*

TED: Just a little joke.

The reaction on their faces says all.

[*Sheepish*] Wasn't… wasn't that a good idea?

Lights fade out.

We hear MICHAEL *singing in a flat and toneless voice.*

MICHAEL: [*sung*] What's new Pussycat? Woooo-ooh-ooooh… What's new Pussycat? Wooo-oooh-oooh-oooh.

On the last note MICHAEL's *toneless voice goes flat.*

THE END

www.currency.com.au

Visit Currency Press' website now to:

- Buy your books online
- Browse through our full list of titles, from plays to screenplays, books on theatre, film and music, and more
- Choose a play for your school or amateur performance group by cast size and gender
- Obtain information about performance rights
- Find out about theatre productions and other performing arts news across Australia
- For students, read our study guides
- For teachers, access syllabus and other relevant information
- Sign up for our email newsletter

The performing arts publisher

www.ingramcontent.com/pod-product-compliance
Lightning Source LLC
Chambersburg PA
CBHW040307170426
43194CB00022B/2923